EXPLORING KAMAKURA

Michael Cooper

EXPLORING KAMAKURA

A Guide for the Curious Traveler

New York · WEATHERHILL · *Tokyo*

First edition, 1979

Published by John Weatherhill, Inc., of New York and Tokyo, with editorial offices at 7-6-13 Roppongi, Minato-ku, Tokyo 106, Japan. Protected by copyright under terms of the International Copyright Union; all rights reserved. Printed in Japan.

ISBN 0-8348-0144-2

For Barbara

Contents

Map Following Page 160

Foreword

IN GRANDEUR, CULTURAL RICHES, and historical interest, Kamakura is admittedly not in the same class as Kyoto. Perhaps it may best be described as a mini-Kyoto. But it has a charm of its own, and being relatively small in size, a great deal of the city can be seen in one day, while its location near Tokyo makes it a convenient and accessible place for sightseeing, excursions, and hiking. What a boon Kamakura can be for the hard-pressed host and hostess when friends arrive for a brief stopover and ask to be shown something of "old Japan."

Unfortunately, many foreign visitors get to see just two or three temples and shrines, and come away with little or no idea of the local history and legends. So this booklet has been compiled to help such people gain a better appreciation of this fascinating place called Kamakura.

The city is reputed to possess no less than sixty-five Buddhist temples and nineteen Shinto shrines, and it is, of course, impossible to cover all these institutions in a small book. Instead, the purpose of this guide is to provide visitors with some general information about the principal places of interest. And thus the reader is spared long lists of dates, names, statistics, and other scholarly impedimenta, which would only serve to confuse rather than enlighten. There also seemed little point in writing about places and works of art that are not accessible to the ordinary visitor.

In any account of Kamakura's ancient monuments, it is not always easy to distinguish between historical fact and fanciful legend, and often enough the latter is an embroidered version of the former. So when recounting stories about Kamakura's past, I have not always troubled to interject qualifying phrases such as "According to legend" and "It is said that." For this I make no apology, as this is a small book to be enjoyed as an amiable companion and not studied as a scholarly text.

Kamakura can be easily reached from Tokyo and Yokohama by the Yokosuka Line (Japan National Railways). The journey takes exactly one hour from Tokyo Station and 28 minutes from Yokohama Station. This train runs down the Tokaidō Line until it reaches Ōfuna Station, where it branches down the Miura Peninsula. The first stop after Ōfuna is Kita-Kamakura Station, and you should get off here when visiting the temples of North Kamakura (Chapter 3). The next stop, Kamakura Station, is only four more minutes down the line, and this is where you get off to visit the other areas of the town.

There are two ways of getting to Enoshima by public transportation. You can catch the Enoshima Line at Kamakura Station, and this will take you to Enoshima Station in 22 minutes. Alternatively, you can utilize the private Odakyū Line that starts from Shinjuku Station in Tokyo and takes 75 minutes. Take care to catch an Enoshima-bound train, for most of the trains on this line run to Odawara and will not take you to Enoshima.

In the text of this book, the suffixes -ji, -in, and -dera refer to Buddhist temples. The names of Japanese people living before the Meiji era (1868–1912) are written in traditional order—that is, family name first, personal name second. Post-Meiji names are given in Western order—personal name first, family name second.

In the back of this booklet there is a foldout map showing all the locations described and numbering them consecutively in the order in which they are discussed. Except for the "Kita-Kamakura" chapter, for which the tour begins from Kita-Kamakura Station, and those in the "Hills to the West," "Great Buddha," and "Enoshima and the Way Thither" chapters, which start from the west exit (*nishiguchi*) of Kamakura Station, the tours all begin at the east exit (*higashiguchi*) of Kamakura Station.

For the convenience of the traveler, the names of all locations are given in both romanized form and Japanese characters at the beginning of each chapter, along with the approximate walking (or, in some instances, riding) times between the places listed. For those people who don't speak Japanese, it will be easiest when asking directions in Kamakura to show the characters for the place in question. These characters will also be convenient for those who want to ask directions about buses, of which there are many available, or who choose to use taxis, although in both cases you should be forewarned that traffic snarls in Kamakura can, depending on the time of day and the day of the week, slow vehicular movement to a snail's pace.

In some cases it will be necessary to retrace your steps partially when moving from one sight to another on a tour. This is unavoidable, but the order in which I have listed the various places is actually the best one to follow for each tour. This does not mean, however, that this order has to be strictly adhered to; depending on the time available and the inclination of the visitor, parts of the tours can be cut or mixed to tailor each program to individual convenience or taste. Whatever the case, Kamakura has a wide variety of pleasures and sights, and I hope that you will enjoy and make the most of your visit there.

History

"WE DYNED THIS DAY at a towne called Camacra, which in tymes past (500 years since) was the greatest cittie of Japon," reported the English merchant Richard Cocks in his diary on 18 October 1616. He went on to add that the place had "divers pagodas very sumptuose. . . . I never did see such pleasant walkes amongst pyne and spruce trees as are about these pagodas, espetially 5 of them more renowned then the rest."

The visitor to Kamakura today can still enjoy the pleasant walks among the pine trees between the different temples, but it may be difficult to visualize how this town, with a population at present of about 160,000, could have once been "the greatest cittie of Japon." Admittedly Cocks is guilty of some exaggeration here, but it remains true that seven centuries ago Kamakura was in fact the military and administrative center of Japan. To understand just how this came about, we must delve into its history and trace the developments that brought this small town into such prominence.

In the beginning of their recorded history, the people of Japan were divided up into various large clans occupying the western and central regions of the country. Gradually the power and authority of the Yamato clan increased until it controlled most of the central regions. In the course of time a centralized state was set up and the rulers of the Yamato clan became the first emperors of Japan. In 792 Kyoto was chosen as the site for the new capital, and it was there that the emperor established his court and ruled the country.

During the tenth century, however, the role of the emperor was increasingly relegated to the religious and cultural spheres, and real political power was wielded by a succession of regents drawn from the all-powerful Fujiwara family. Court life reached the height of its glittering splendor around the year 1000 (this was when the famous novel *Genji monogatari* was written), and the capital was the center of culture, art, and refined living. The eastern regions of the country were occupied by military families, whom the court nobility regarded as uncouth and boorish. But as the prestige of the Fujiwara inevitably began to wane, it became necessary to call on the tough warrior families to put down uprisings and preserve order, and the political importance of the military class grew.

There were two leading warrior clans, the Taira and the Minamoto, and these two families began an all-out struggle for supremacy. At first the Taira forces were successful, and under the leadership of Taira Kiyomori they controlled the court and the capital. In 1159 Kiyomori inflicted a shattering defeat on the rival clan. Its leader, Minamoto Yoshitomo, and two of his sons were killed, while other members of his family fell into Taira hands.

Among the prisoners was Yoshitomo's third son, the thirteen-year-old Yoritomo, and it was naturally assumed that he too would be put to death. But the boy's life was spared at the intercession of Kiyomori's mother, and he was sent off to live in a temple on the Izu Peninsula. At the same time, Yoshitsune, a younger half brother of Yoritomo's, was banished to a temple near Kyoto. This uncharacteristic act of mercy on the part of Kiyomori was to result in the downfall of his family and the triumph of his detested rivals, the Minamoto.

The spirited Yoritomo was obviously not meant for a peaceful, prayerful life in a temple, and by 1180 he was busily gathering support for his Minamoto family among local warriors in the Kantō region of eastern Japan, where there were men still loyal to the memory of his late father. Once he felt he was strong enough to resume the military struggle against the Taira, Yoritomo had to decide where he would set up his headquarters, and Kamakura was an obvious choice.

The area had a long history, for in the seventh century Fujiwara Kamatari, the founder of the illustrious Fujiwara clan, is said to have visited the region and, as a result of a dream, he enshrined his *kama* (a short sword or a sickle) there. The place thus became known as Kama-kura, or the sickle storehouse. This legend conveniently provides a romantic explanation for the origin of the city's name, although in fact the name may well be derived from the first part of Kamatari's own name. Alternatively, it has been plausibly suggested that it comes from an old Ainu word meaning, appropriately enough, "the place of the crossed hills." Whatever the origin of the place name, Yoriyoshi, one of Yoritomo's ancestors, settled in the locality in 1063 and erected there a shrine dedicated to Hachiman, the patron deity of the Minamoto clan.

A seasoned warrior himself, Yoritomo was anxious to set up his headquarters far from the debilitating and effeminate court atmosphere of Kyoto. His family owned estates in the Kantō region, where Kamakura was located, and could count on the support of local military families. In addition to these considerations, Kamakura was an ideal choice as a military headquarters. Surrounded by hills on three sides and by the sea on the fourth, the place had natural strategic value and could be easily defended from attack. Thus, in December 1180 Yoritomo led his troops into Kamakura, establishing his headquarters there.

After some initial setbacks, Yoritomo's fortunes began to prosper. In 1184, thanks largely to a surprise attack led by the dashing Yoshitsune, his troops won a major battle at Ichinotani, near present-day Kobe, and in the following year the naval victory at Dannoura, in the Shimonoseki Straits between Honshu and Kyushu, finally established Yoritomo as the undisputed military ruler of Japan.

In this way the feudal period of Japanese history began and the

Painting of Minamoto Yoritomo, done in the late twelfth to early thirteenth century. Courtesy of Jingo-ji, Kyoto.

government of the country effectively remained in military hands from that time until the Meiji Restoration in 1868. Officially the emperor, who resided in Kyoto, was the ruler of the land, and Yoritomo, the shogun, merely acted in his name. In practice, however, although due deference was usually paid to the throne, political and military power was firmly based in Kamakura, and whether they liked it or not, both emperor and courtiers were obliged to conform to the wishes of the bakufu, or military government. Thanks to Yoritomo's choice of headquarters, the small town of Kamakura became "the greatest cittie of Japon," and the Kamakura period stretches from 1192 (when Yoritomo was appointed shogun) to 1333, thus forming a major epoch in Japanese political and art history.

Despite Yoritomo's having firmly established his leadership, dissension was rife in the new government, and family quarrels among the Minamoto led to death and bloodshed. Yoshitsune had been largely instrumental in gaining the victories against the Taira armies, and he had been congratulated and honored by the Kyoto court on his military success. This may well have been an astute move on the part of the emperor to divide the Minamoto leadership, and if it was, it certainly succeeded, for Yoritomo's suspicions were aroused by the honors awarded to Yoshitsune. When the latter, escorting important Taira prisoners, reached Kamakura in 1185, he was refused permission to enter the city. Despite Yoshitsune's moving letter declaring his innocence of any plot and begging his brother to restore him to his friendship, Yoritomo would not relent and even sent a band of soldiers to murder his younger brother.

Thus began the saga, so often featured in Noh, Kabuki, and film, of the gallant, persecuted Yoshitsune fleeing from place to place to escape the vengeful wrath of his jealous brother, until finally, in 1189, at the age of thirty, Yoshitsune, trapped by his enemies, committed suicide in order to avoid capture.

Another colorful personality belonging to Yoritomo's immediate family was his wife, Masako, reputed to be the strongest-willed woman in the whole of Japanese history. This is not a claim to be made lightly, but various episodes in Masako's life would seem to qualify her for this title. On hearing, for example, that her husband had been dallying with a lover, Masako promptly had the girl's house burned to the ground. And when, in 1184, Yoritomo ordered the execution of his son-in-law, the infuriated Masako later prevailed on her husband to have the executioner put to death, although the poor man had only carried out his lord's command.

Yoritomo's career came to an end in 1199, when he was thrown from his horse and died shortly thereafter. Owing to his unexpected death, practical plans for his succession had not been drawn up, and the Kamakura government faced a major crisis. On her husband's death, the formidable Masako dutifully shaved her head and became a nun, but she remained very much in the center of political power, thus earning for herself the nickname of Ama Shōgun—the Nun Shogun. Together with her father, Hōjō Tokimasa, she formed a council to continue the government, while Yoritomo's eldest son, eighteen-year-old Yoriie, was officially appointed shogun.

But an opposing faction forced the young man to resign and become a monk in 1203; in the following year he was assassinated, probably at the instigation of his grandfather Hōjō Tokimasa. Yoriie's place was taken by Sanetomo, his twelve-year-old brother, a boy given more to poetry than to military affairs, and he in turn was assassinated in 1219 by one of his nephews. When we recall that Yoritomo had also exiled and put to death Noriyori, another of his half brothers, in 1193, it is clear that relationships within the Minamoto family were not always of the most cordial type and left something to be desired.

Neither Yoriie nor Sanetomo left any male heirs, and in the ensuing power struggle Masako saw to it that political administration was taken over by her own Hōjō family. The family did not assume the title of shogun, an office that from then onward was usually occupied by a youthful and quite ineffectual aristocrat, sometimes only two or three years of age. Instead they adopted the rank of *shikken,* or regent to the young shogun. Thus arose a very peculiar administrative system. In theory the emperor residing in Kyoto ruled the land, but in practice power rested in the hands of a regent who acted on behalf of a young and ineffective military commander.

Despite this apparent complexity, the system worked reasonably well, and the Hōjō family produced a number of able rulers. In 1221 a former emperor tried to regain his imperial rights, but his army was decisively beaten by the Kamakura troops. The Hōjō family then asserted its authority in a businesslike way by deposing the three-year-old reigning emperor and packing three retired emperors off to different places of exile. To prevent any further disturbances from that quarter, Hōjō deputies were stationed in Kyoto to administer the city and keep a watchful eye on the activities of the court. As a result, no further trouble was experienced from among the nobles, and relations between Kamakura and Kyoto actually became quite cordial.

With their leadership firmly established, the Hōjō rulers had leisure and inclination to turn to religion and culture. The fifth and sixth regents, Tokiyori and Tokimune, patronized Buddhism lavishly and invited eminent Chinese monks to settle in Kamakura and establish monasteries. To this day the city is still an important center of Zen Buddhism. These new temples and monasteries required religious statues, and Kamakura-period sculpture is characterized by a certain manly vigor appropriate to the military atmosphere of the Hōjō capital.

A leading religious figure of this time was the famous patriarch Nichiren, who lived and preached in Kamakura for a number of years. He fell foul of the Hōjō government when he threatened the country with divine wrath unless people adopted his religious message, and he was sent off to exile at Itō in Izu in 1260. Pardoned within three years, Nichiren returned to Kamakura, only to inveigh once more against rival sects; this time he was banished to the lonely island of Sado by the exasperated Hōjōs.

But Nichiren's prophecies of doom seemed to have been fulfilled when in 1274 and 1281 the great Kublai Khan sent his Mongol soldiers to invade Japan. Both attacks on Hakata, in Kyushu, were beaten off, thanks largely to the timely arrival of typhoons, which were regarded as *kamikaze,* or divine winds, by the hard-pressed defenders. Although the Hōjōs had successfully thrown back the invaders, the cost involved in the military operations and in maintaining defenses in Kyushu until Kublai Khan died in 1294 sapped the strength and vitality of the bakufu. Normally after a victorious campaign, troops were rewarded with booty and land; in this case there was neither booty nor land to bestow on them, and dissatisfaction with the ruling Hōjōs began to spread.

The prestige of the Kamakura government was further lowered when the quality of the Hōjō leadership started to decline. Hōjō Takatoki became the ninth regent in 1311 at the tender age of eight, and administrative power was largely taken over by his ministers. Takatoki neglected his official duties in favor of attending dancing performances and dog fights; he became so enamored of the latter pastime that his vassal lords were ordered to present suitable dogs, the champions among which were reverently carried around in litters.

In contrast to the dissipated Takatoki, the throne was at that time occupied by an energetic emperor, Go-Daigo, who decided that the time had come to reassert imperial authority. He was banished in 1332 because of his opposition to the Kamakura government, but escaped from exile in the following year. The bakufu sent a powerful army, under the command of Ashikaga Takauji, to Kyoto, but this astute general, seeing which way the wind was blowing, switched his allegiance and declared for the emperor.

Encouraged by this turn of events, Go-Daigo dispatched loyalist troops against Kamakura, and in July 1333 they fought their way into the city and seized the Hōjō headquarters. After five days of bitter fighting the defenders could no longer offer any further resistance. Takatoki and hundreds of his followers committed mass suicide, and the Kamakura period of Japanese history came to a violent and abrupt end.

Political power was then transferred back to Kyoto, although the hapless emperor did not enjoy it for very long. Within a few years he had once more become a mere figurehead, with the real power and authority in the hands of Takauji, the first of the fifteen Ashikaga shoguns.

Deprived of its former importance, Kamakura rapidly declined in status, although for a while it still remained the government headquarters for eastern Japan. But even this relatively minor role was lost when the castle town of Odawara rose to prominence in the sixteenth century. Kamakura was sacked and pillaged in both 1455 and 1526. In addition to these man-made disasters, natural calamities such as earthquakes, fires, floods, and typhoons periodically took their toll; the listing of these misfortunes occupies several closely printed pages in accounts of Kamakura's history. Even Richard Cocks, in his brief visit, heard something about the city's troubled past. "Som report this cittie to be destroid with fire and brimston; but I enquired of the enhabetantes, and they say they never heard of any such matter but only that it was burned and ruenated by war."

At the beginning of the seventeenth century, the new bakufu established by the Tokugawa family set up its administrative center in Edo (present-day Tokyo), and the Tōkaidō road linking Edo with Kyoto became the most-traveled route in the country. But this road ran to the north of Kamakura, thus bypassing the old city. And so Kamakura became little more than a fishing village, with only dreams and monuments of its former splendor. As Cocks noted: "But at present, it is no cittie, but scattared howses seated heare and theare."

It was, in fact, only in 1889, when the Yokosuka railway line was completed, that the city's fortunes began to revive. As a result of this convenient rail link, Kamakura has grown into a bedroom town for office workers commuting to Yokohama and Tokyo. And blessed with a mild climate owing to its sheltered location, the place has also become a popular tourist resort where visitors can enjoy not only swimming, surfing, and yachting in the bay, but also visiting the ancient temples and monuments testifying to the city's past greatness. Further, it is now a cultural center in its own right and a favorite residence for artists and authors.

Hachiman Shrine

Kamakura ___15 min.___→ Hachiman Shrine
Station   鶴岡八幡宮

HACHIMAN SHRINE Hachiman Shrine (or, in Japanese, Hachiman-gū) so dominates Kamakura, both from its central location and the variety of cultural activities organized there, that most of this chapter will be devoted to the shrine and the legends attached to it.

As noted earlier, the shrine is said to have been founded in 1063 by Minamoto Yoriyoshi near the seashore (a stone marker indicates the original site), and it was only natural that it should have been dedicated to Hachiman, the tutelary deity of the Minamoto clan. Hachiman is usually regarded today as the god of war, but in fact his role seems to have changed through the course of centuries, for in earlier times he was recognized more as a guardian deity of the Japanese nation. Actually, Hachiman is the apotheosis of Emperor Ōjin who, by traditional count, died in 310 and enjoyed a particularly peaceful reign. Perhaps he is regarded as the god of war because his pregnant mother, Jingō, was carrying him in her womb when she led a military expedition against Korea.

Yoritomo established his headquarters in Kamakura in 1180. In the same year he had the ancestral shrine transferred to an imposing site at the top of the main Kamakura valley on a hill called Tsurugaoka (Stork Mound); hence, to distinguish this shrine from other Hachiman shrines located in different parts of the country, its full formal name is Tsurugaoka Hachiman-gū. Yoritomo often worshiped at this shrine and took a keen interest in its maintenance and development. It is recorded, for example, that he went to Hachiman for a service on 15 May 1181 and, noticing the weeds and brambles growing in the precincts, commanded that the shrine be cleaned up. When Yoritomo gave orders, everybody jumped, and the grounds were tidied up on the very same day.

In the following year his wife, Masako, was found to be pregnant, and Yoritomo decreed that an avenue be constructed from the seashore through the center of the city right up to Hachiman Shrine so that the baby could be carried in fitting state for a dedication ceremony. Work on the road was completed by 19 April, and the wide avenue linking seashore with shrine is one of Kamakura's most impressive and durable landmarks. Masako gave birth to Yoriie, Yoritomo's eldest son, on 14 July, and the avenue is still called Wakamiya Ōji, or Young Prince Avenue; so although Yoriie did not enjoy a very long or distinguished career, his memory is kept alive by this central road.

The avenue is crossed at intervals by three massive *torii,* or Shinto archways, and between the middle one and the one immediately in front of the shrine, an embankment lined with cherry trees runs along the center of the road. This provides a splendid sight at the beginning of April when the trees are in full bloom, although the crowds that come to admire the colorful spectacle make tranquil and leisurely blossom-viewing all but impossible.

Incidentally, the narrow road called Komachi-dōri, running parallel to the left of the main avenue (as you walk toward the shrine), is well worth strolling through. At one time a nondescript thoroughfare, in recent years it has become an attractive pedestrian lane, traffic-free on weekends and holidays, full of antique and folkcraft shops, boutiques, and restaurants.

Both on this side street and Wakamiya Ōji there are a number of shops specializing in a local product called *Kamakura-bori,* or Kamakura carving. This type of woodwork is said to have flourished in Kamakura with the establishment of the great Zen temples there in the thirteenth century, when wooden incense boxes and trays were required for Buddhist liturgical purposes. The decoration was originally Chinese in inspiration, but in the course of time Japanese motifs began to be used in the designs.

With the government's patronage of Shinto shrines and the decline of Buddhist temples in the second half of the nineteenth century, carvers who had specialized in religious goods switched their attention to making tea trays, saucers, mirror frames, and other everyday objects, and it is generally these items that make up Kamakura carving today. The Gotō and Mitsuhashi, both claiming descent from Unkei, the celebrated sculptor of the Kamakura period, are the two principal families producing this fine work today. What makes their goods so attractive is not only the graceful design carved into the tray, but also the skillful application of seven or eight layers of lacquer, which imparts a rich reddish glow and, at the same time, protects the wood from damage.

At the entrance of the shrine precincts is a decorative red bridge, called either Drum Bridge or Red Bridge, first built on this spot in 1182. The less agile or more prudent visitor can avoid this obstacle by walking around on either side. It is said that passage over this steeply curved bridge was formerly reserved exclusively for the shogun, but it is difficult to see how he could have gone up one side and down the other without losing much of his shogunal dignity. In the same year as this bridge was first built, Yoritomo gave orders for rice fields in front of the shrine to be converted into lotus ponds. On Masako's suggestion, three islands were constructed in the large right-hand pond and four in the smaller left-hand one.

The point of the exercise is somewhat subtle and probably escapes the attention of most tourists. "Three" in Japanese is *san,* which also means birth and prosperity, while "four" is pronounced *shi,* meaning death and downfall. Thus the right-hand pond represented the triumph of the Minamoto clan, while that on the left pointed to the melancholy fate of the rival Taira family. As a result, the two ponds (actually, there is only one, for the two parts are joined by the stream running beneath the Drum Bridge) are known as the Gempei (that is, Minamoto-Taira) Pond.

The main avenue running through the shrine grounds is cut at right-angles by a straight, dirt-covered track, and it is along here that *yabusame,* or mounted archery, takes place every year. Yoritomo spared no effort to keep his warriors in training, organizing hunting expeditions on the slopes of Mount Fuji, archery practice on the Kamakura beach, and, from 1187, mounted archery here in the shrine precincts. A display of mounted archery is put on at Hachiman on 16 September, and it is well worth viewing. The only trouble is that the large number of spectators makes it hard to get a good, uninterrupted view of the spectacle. One solution to this problem is to come early in the morning and watch in uncrowded comfort the horsemen galloping down the 150-meter track on practice runs.

The actual formal display is preceded by a grand procession of shrine officials and of mounted archers, dressed in the hunting costume of the Kamakura period and carrying long bows. When this parade has finished, one by one the riders thunder down the avenue, from east to west, holding on to their horses by their legs only and letting off three arrows in quick succession at wooden targets. If they successfully hit the target (and they generally do), a shrine maiden waves a decorated wand to signify the hit.

A little further along the main avenue, the visitor reaches a wide open space located immediately below the broad flight of steps running up to the shrine buildings. In the middle of this compound is a red-painted roofed dancing platform, and this commemorates one of the most famous and dramatic dances in Japanese history. It has already been mentioned that the vengeful Yoritomo began hunting down his half brother Yoshitsune. The shogun's troops never managed to capture him alive, but the fugitive's lover,

Hachiman Shrine, showing the dance stage on the left, the famous gingko tree in the center, and the steps leading up to the main shrine.

Shizuka Gozen, a former Kyoto dancer, was made a prisoner and brought to Kamakura. The girl's dancing skill was well known, and she was invited, or rather commanded, to perform a dance at Hachiman Shrine. Shizuka reluctantly agreed and went.

On seeing Yoritomo seated behind curtains of state, Shizuka defiantly sang a song in praise of her fugitive lover, Yoshitsune. Yoritomo was not amused and spared the girl's life only at the intercession of Masako. But when Shizuka was soon afterward found to be bearing Yoshitsune's child, the shogun gave instructions that the baby, if a boy, was to be killed. The dancer eventually gave birth to a baby boy and the infant was put to death in compliance with Yoritomo's orders.

Such a dramatic event could never be allowed to be forgotten in Japan, and every year during the spring festival an accomplished dancer mounts the platform in the shrine grounds and performs a classical dance in commemoration of Shizuka's act of defiance. The tragic fate of Shizuka's baby is also kept alive in the traditional theater. In these adaptations, as the time of birth approaches, the dramatic tension builds up—if the baby is a girl, her life will be spared, but no mercy will be shown to a boy. Happily, in at least one drama version, the warrior appointed to kill the child cannot bring himself to carry out such a cruel command and allows the baby to float away in the sea in a basket, Moses-like, and, needless to say, the infant survives. But according to *Yoshitsune,* a fifteenth-century chronicle, the baby is not spared and is brutally put to death on Kamakura beach.

To the right of the steps are located two small shrines, the first being called Wakamiya (and it is believed that it was in this shrine that Shizuka performed her celebrated dance) and the second Shirahata. This latter name means White Flag, white being the color of the Minamoto banner, and the shrine is dedicated to the memory of Yoritomo and his second son, Sanetomo.

Between these two subshrines may be seen two sizeable boulders, and these are noteworthy relics, as Benkei used to lightly play ball with them. This introduces yet another colorful personage— Benkei, the devoted retainer of Yoshitsune. Although the son of a monk and a monk himself, Benkei would not appear to have been cut out for contemplative monastic existence. He used to amuse himself by waylaying passersby at night as they crossed Gojō Bridge in Kyoto and relieving them of their swords. Hoping to increase his collection of swords to the round number of one thousand, he challenged the youthful Yoshitsune one night and to his surprise was beaten in the ensuing duel.

From then onward Benkei was Yoshitsune's faithful servant, and on more than one occasion he saved his fugitive master's life not only through his immense strength but also through his quick wits. As we see in the Noh play *Ataka* and its Kabuki version *Kanjinchō,* Yoshitsune on one occasion tries to slip through a checkpoint while disguised as a humble servant. The commander of the barrier scrutinizes him closely, but his suspicions are allayed when the quick-witted Benkei stalks up and strikes the disguised Yoshitsune with his staff, berating him for his laziness. No ordinary retainer would ever dream of behaving in such outrageous fashion toward his lord and master, and so the party is allowed to proceed, and Yoshitsune's life is once more spared.

To the left of the broad flight of steps leading to the main shrine buildings is an impressive old gingko tree, and it was here that Yoritomo's second son, Sanetomo, was assassinated on a snowy day in 1219 when his disgruntled nephew leaped out from behind the tree and cut off his head. There is a certain amount of amicable controversy whether this is the actual tree (which would make the gingko at least eight hundred years old) or whether the present tree is merely the successor of the one from behind which the murderer jumped out in 1219. Whichever it is, there is no denying that the towering tree is certainly very old indeed; the best time to view it is mid-November when its bright yellow leaves form a gloriously colorful spectacle by the side of the steps.

Sanetomo is generally depicted as a rather romantic character, and historical evidence does indeed support this view. He was no mean poet and in fact corresponded with the leading poet of the day, Fujiwara Teika. Legend has added extra pathos to his tragic end. The young shogun (he was only twenth-six years old at the time of his death) had been warned that an attempt on his life might be made when he paid a ceremonial visit to the shrine at the New Year. His attendant begs him to wear protective armor beneath his formal robes. The young lord refuses to take this precaution, but cuts a lock from his hair and leaves it to his weeping servant as a memento. Before setting out, he writes a final poem and then goes resignedly to his death. As he was walking down the snow-covered steps of the shrine, his embittered nephew emerged from behind the gingko and lopped off his head. The assassin was soon captured and executed, but Sanetomo's head was never found.

The vermilion-painted shrine, renovated in 1828, comes as

something of an anticlimax when finally reached at the top of the steps. Two guardian deities, Yadaijin and Sadaijin (the counterparts of the Niō guardian kings in front of Buddhist temples), protect the shrine from malign influences, but otherwise no other statues are to be seen. Like most Shinto shrines, the interior of the central hall is practically bare and devoid of decoration. Babies in arms are carried inside by their parents for a form of dedication service, but apart from this, no other activity can usually be discerned.

To the left-rear of the main hall is a gallery in which are exhibited *mikoshi* (portable shrines), masks, weapons, robes, and other items, but the display holds little of interest for the ordinary visitor. According to an old guidebook, the shrine possesses a somewhat remarkable relic in the form of the skull of Yoritomo as a young man, but repeated and diligent inquiries on my part have so far failed to track down this intriguing item. If this object were ever discovered, it would undoubtedly prove to be of considerable historical, cultural, and scientific interest.

MUSEUM OF MODERN ART To the left of the main avenue running through the shrine grounds is located the contemporary building that houses the Museum of Modern Art, an enterprising institution that stages frequent exhibitions of both Japanese and Western art. On the other side of the avenue is to be found the Kokuhōkan, or Hall of National Treasures, founded in 1928 and built after the style of the Shōsō-in treasure house in Nara.

KOKUHŌKAN A visit to the Kokuhōkan is a must for anybody interested in the art of the Kamakura period. Many of the temples in and around the city possess fine examples of paintings and statues, but more often than not these are not kept on public display, and it is difficult, even for a person speaking Japanese, to view them without a good deal of preliminary and long-drawn-out negotiations. Even then, the inadequate lighting and positioning of these works of art in the temples often prevent full appreciation.

But here in the museum, superb examples of Kamakura statues, on loan from local temples, are excellently displayed in ideal conditions, enabling the visitor to get some idea of the power and vigor of Kamakura statuary. A booklet, illustrated with good monochrome photographs and written in indifferent English, is available for the foreign visitor. In the museum's one large chamber you can admire the famous statue of Uesugi Shigefusa dressed in formal court robes; Jizō, the guardian deity of children, seated on a lotus; three fearsome judges from hell (one dated 1261); ten emaciated disciples of the Buddha (1258); and a realistic depiction of Eisai, who introduced Zen (and tea) into Japan.

On the pictorial side, the Kokuhōkan possesses on loan a valuable collection of paintings (the best-known one probably being the portrait of Tao Lung, the founder of Kenchō-ji temple; see page 34), but pride of place must be given to its medieval *emaki,* or illustrated scrolls. The most outstanding example is undoubtedly the thirteenth-century *Taima Mandala,* a beautiful depiction of a legend concerning the cult of Amida Buddha. I was fortunate enough on one occasion to be permitted to make a detailed inspection of this masterpiece in a private room within the museum. Two other scrolls worth noting are the *Jōdo Goso* (1306) and *Hasedera Engi* (1557). Unlike the statues, however, the pictures and scrolls are not on permanent display.

The early Kamakura period contains many colorful personalities—Yoritomo, Masako, Yoshitsune, Benkei, Shizuka, and Sanetomo, to mention just the principal ones—and drama and legend have preserved, and probably enhanced, their memory to this day. Each year during Kamakura's spring festival a long procession of local inhabitants dressed up as warriors and courtiers starts from the beach and wends its way to Hachiman Shrine.

Many of the historical characters are identifiable by their names inscribed on an accompanying banner.

Yoritomo is dressed in magnificent armor, and, although he is sometimes riding a less than robust horse, he has the leading role, for he was, after all, the founding lord of Kamakura. His half brother, the ever-popular and gallant Yoshitsune, follows close behind on horseback, guarded by the faithful Benkei, clad as a soldier-monk, wearing elevated clogs, and carrying a *naginata,* or halbert, ready to protect his master to the end. Amid a retinue of brightly robed ladies-in-waiting, Masako is carried in a litter through the streets in stately fashion, with the beautiful Shizuka coming not far behind. All of these historical characters lived more than seven hundred years ago, yet their memory remains un-diminished and undimmed in Kamakura (and, for that matter, elsewhere in Japan) to this very day.

In addition to the celebrations held in the spring and autumn festivals, various other colorful events take place at the shrine throughout the year. On and around the 7-5-3 festival (15 November), children of these three ages are brought to the shrine wearing kimono and other traditional costumes.

In recent years Hachiman Shrine has become a popular drawing point at New Year's, attracting more than 1.5 million people during the first three days of the year. Traffic is banned from the center of the city, and it's fun to join the good-humored, orderly crowds converging on the shrine to ask for good fortune in the coming year. But I won't spoil this happy picture by describing the packed state of public transport bearing the people into and out of the city. . . .

Kita-Kamakura

Kita-Kamakura ——*5 min.*——→ Engaku-ji ——*10 min.*——→
Station   円覚寺

Tōkei-ji ——*10 min.*——→ Jōchi-ji ——*15 min.*——→
東慶寺   浄智寺

Meigetsu-in ——*20 min.*——→ Kenchō-ji ——*10 min.*——→ Ennō-ji
明月院   建長寺   円応寺

THE AREA COVERED in this chapter is really northwest Kamakura, but as the district is called Kita (North) Kamakura and the station serving it is Kita-Kamakura Station, it is perhaps less confusing to refer to it simply as North Kamakura. Just as East Kamakura is the stronghold of Nichiren temples, so this area is characterized by its Rinzai Zen foundations.

ENGAKU-JI   Of all these Zen temples, Engaku-ji is easily the most accessible, as it lies alongside Kita-Kamakura Station. In fact the railway line has cut through part of the temple's original property, for the rustic pond and trees on the other side of the tracks once belonged to the monastery. The pond is called the White Heron Pond, for when the founder of Engaku-ji came to Kamakura in the thirteenth century, he was led to the present site by a flock of white herons that flew down onto the pond and thus showed him where to establish the temple.

Engaku-ji is the second of Kamakura's *Gozan,* or Five Mountains temples, the five principal Rinzai Zen foundations in the city. This term is not peculiar to Kamakura, for Kyoto also has its Five Mountains temples; to go further afield, there were also five such institutions in China, from where the label Five Mountains originally came. Richard Cocks must have heard something about this grouping of temples, for he noted, as you may recall, that there were in Kamakura various "pagodas, espetially 5 of them more renowned then the rest."

Zen Buddhism in Japan is divided into two main schools, Rinzai and Sōtō. The former tends to place emphasis in its training on the use of the koan, an enigmatic or rationally unanswerable riddle (for example, "Two hands clapping make a sound. What is the sound of one hand?"), which, when solved, leads to abrupt enlightenment. The famous scholar Daisetz Suzuki was an adherent of this Rinzai school (he in fact lived in Kita-Kamakura until he died in 1966 at the patriarchal age of 96), and as a result of his widely read English-language books on Zen, this school is better known in Western countries than is its companion Sōtō school. The Sōtō school, on the other hand, advocates a more gradual process of enlightenment, and despite the fame of Rinzai abroad, the members of the Sōtō branch are more numerous in Japan.

Engaku-ji was founded in 1282 by the regent Hōjō Tokimune. He himself was a fervent member of the Zen sect, and it is said that he founded the monastery so that the monks could pray for the soldiers killed in the second Mongol invasion attempt of the previous year. In general, most of the Hōjō rulers favored Zen more than any other Buddhist sect, for it was felt that the mental discipline required of Zen disciples was peculiarly suitable for warriors. Tokimune was fortunate in obtaining the services of a distinguished Chinese monk, Wu-hsueh Tsu-yuan (better known by his posthumous Japanese title, Bukkō Kokushi), as the

The main gate of Engaku-ji.

foundation's first abbot. At that time there were in Japan quite a number of monks who had taken refuge from China after the fall of the Sung dynasty in 1279. The newly introduced Zen sect received a rather frigid reception in Kyoto from some of the long-established temples, so the refugee monks tended to gather in the less conservative climate of Kamakura.

Like so many other monastic foundations in Kamakura, Engaku-ji has seen more prosperous times, and visitors today can get little idea of its former splendor unless they consult old plans of the temple grounds. But the great *sanmon,* or main gate, at the top of the first flight of steps gives some indication of Engaku-ji's past grandeur. It was reconstructed in 1780 and houses statues of Kannon and the Rakan (the Buddha's immediate disciples). In former days you could clamber up a rather shaky ladder to inspect these, but nowadays the interior of the gate, like other parts of the temple grounds, are off-limits to the ordinary visitor. This is also true of an interesting series of caves and grottoes, to the left of the gate, through which you used to be able to wander at will.

The long flight of steps to the right, however, leads up the hillside to an ancient relic that is still accessible. At the top of the 137 steps (the habit of counting steps when visiting Kamakura temples is a hard one to break) is Engaku-ji's great bell, the largest in Kamakura. Cast in 1301, it is over 2.5 meters in height and has a beautiful, mellow sound when rung. As was his wont, the writer Lafcadio Hearn waxed enthusiastically about this particular bell. On his visit to Engaku-ji in 1891, he rang the bell himself, and it produced "a sound as deep as thunder, extraordinary, yet beautiful," duly followed by "another and lesser and sweeter billowing of tone." Even after he had finished ringing it, the bell (he tells us) continued to sob and moan for at least ten minutes. Perhaps one would not be prepared to go all the way with this sentimental hyperbole, but it is nevertheless true that the bell does emit a fine sound and, for me, has a most evocative tone.

Visitors to the temple are no longer allowed to ring the bell at will. In fact it is not often rung at all. Easily the best time to listen to this and other temple bells in on the occasion of *kane no joya,* when on New Year's Eve bells throughout the whole country are solemnly rung 108 times, symbolizing the 108 miseries and sufferings of mankind. To enjoy the best and most sonorous effect, it is better not to stand too near a bell, for if you do so, it is inevitable that a certain amount of metalic sound is heard as the wooden beam hits the side of the bronze bell. Instead, it is advisable to station yourself about a mile or so away, and then only the melodious b—o—o—o—o—m can be heard echoing majestically through the night.

This sound is most evocative and moving for Japanese (and for many non-Japanese, as well), for it inevitably brings to mind the famous opening passage of the *Heike monogatari* (the medieval literary account of the fall of the Taira family), where the temple bell tolls the inevitable passing of human glory.

On a somewhat less lofty note, one has to add that a certain amount of commercialism has crept into the New Year's Eve ringing of temple bells. On payment of a fee, visitors stand in line and take turns ringing the bell once. Thus much of the dignity and solemnity of the occasion is lost, especially when it is not unknown for some bell ringers to have anticipated the New Year and to have begun their celebrations somewhat early. Kenchō-ji, another Zen temple in Kita-Kamakura, has stopped this public participation in recent years.

Incidentally, a good view of Tōkei-ji can be obtained from the right of the Benten Shrine behind the Engaku-ji bell. Having toiled up the seemingly endless flights of steps, the visitor can look down over the railway tracks and see the Tōkei-ji buildings nestling harmoniously among the pines and bamboo with a wonderful natural backdrop formed by the wooded hill behind.

The Buddha Hall beyond Engaku-ji's main gate is modern and was completed as recently as 1964. Throughout its long history, the temple has had more than its share of disasters: in 1284, only two years after its foundation, and again in 1526, fire swept through the precincts, destroying most of the buildings, and the Great Kantō Earthquake once more devastated the monastery in 1923. Behind the Buddha Hall are monastery buildings that are not open to casual visitors. About the only time you can enter freely is during the first week of November when the rite of *mushi-boshi* (expel the insects) is held. For two or three days temple treasures—scrolls, paintings, statues, documents—are put on display before being packed away for the winter, and visitors may enter without any formality to view these articles. Kenchō-ji also holds its mushi-boshi on the same days, so the two collections can be conveniently seen at one and the same time.

If you take the path to the left of these monastery buildings, you will pass various subtemples, in some of which sessions of *zazen,* or Zen meditation, are regularly held for the laity. Eventually you will pass by a pond on your left. This is called, rather euphemistically,

Myōkō-ike (The Pond of Sacred Fragrance), and its angular, oblong shape, so uncharacteristic of temple ponds, strongly suggests that it started life as a water cistern before it was elevated to the status of a sacred and fragrant pond.

A path running off to the left above the pond leads to Engaku-ji's most celebrated building, the Shariden, or Relic Hall. You are no longer allowed to enter the courtyard and inspect this small building close up, nor to visit the tomb of the temple's founder located immediately behind it. Not a great deal can be seen from the gate of the courtyard, and to get an idea of what the Shariden really looks like, you must have recourse to illustrated art books.

The building, with its large, heavy roof, is regarded as one of the finest extant examples of Sung-style architecture in Japan and was erected in 1285 by Hōjō Sadatoki, the seventh Kamakura regent. The durability of the hall is attributed to the fact that it houses a sacred relic of the Buddha. Sanetomo, Yoritomo's second son, sent messengers to China asking for the loan of the relic. His request was granted, but the relic was waylaid en route and wound up in Kyoto. But it finally found its way to Kamakura and was enshrined in this building. Recent investigations have shown that the hall has been extensively renovated during the course of its long history, but it nevertheless remains one of the oldest wooden structures in Kamakura.

Further along the main path running up the hillside will be seen an old thatched building set in a pleasant courtyard on the left; this is called the Butsunichian, and it enshrines statues of Tokimune, his son Sadatoki, and his grandson Takatoki (the last of the Hōjō regents). Opposite, on the other side of the path, is a small cave known as the White Deer Cave, for a white deer is said to have emerged from here to listen to the founder's sermon on the day of Engaku-ji's inauguration.

The path finally ends in the garden of a subtemple called Yellow Plum Blossom Temple. The building to the left contains statues of the Zen patriarch Musō Kokushi and Yakushi Nyorai (the Healing

Buddha), while at the end of the garden is a small Kannon shrine.

The grounds of Engaku-ji are an excellent example of how the Zen monks have used the natural beauty of a place to its best advantage, not destroying nature but rather complementing it. The garden mentioned in the last paragraph, for instance, is at the end of a valley and seems to be set in a vast natural amphitheater made up of tree-covered hills. No wonder that Engaku-ji attracts many visitors and that some distinguished people (the historian Sir George Sansom and the novelist Sōseki Natsume, to name just two) chose to live in the temple grounds for a while.

TōKEI-JI   On the other side of the railway tracks from Engaku-ji is situated the famous temple called Tōkei-ji. Exactly why this small temple should be so famous is indicated by the two nick-names it bears—Enkiri-dera (Divorce Temple) and Kakekomi-dera (Run-in Temple).

In olden days in Japan (and, for than matter, in most other countries as well), a man could divorce his wife with very little difficulty or formality. In Japan, all he had to do was draw up and hand her a writ called *mikudarihan* (literally, three-and-a-half lines) and send her back to her family. This right, however, did not extend to the wife, and "women desirous of ending the thrall of connubial woes"* had little choice but to patiently endure their lot. But Tōkei-ji, and a few convents in other parts of the country, offered sanctuary to these poor wives; those who took refuge with the nuns and lived in their community for three (later reduced to two) years were officially considered divorced from their husbands. Hence the popular names accorded to the temple and hence also

---

*This quotation provides me with an opportunity to mention Iso Mutsu's delightful and instructive book, *Kamakura, Fact and Legend*, 1918, 1930, and 1955, unhappily now out of print. English by birth and married to a Japanese diplomat, Mrs. Mutsu obviously had a wide knowledge and deep love of Kamakura, and her book first aroused my own interest in the place.

Tōkei-ji, with its backdrop of hills and trees.

dramatic stories about women seeking sanctuary. It is related, for example, that if a woman, fleeing to the temple with her irate husband in hot pursuit, arrived there at night and found the gate barred, all she had to do was slip off her shoe and toss it over the wall, and she would thereby be regarded as already in sanctuary and inviolate.

The historical truth is a good deal less dramatic. In all probability, relatively few women sought relief from family problems by entering the convent, although no precise figures are available. And it is more than likely that the nuns and authorities did their best to effect a reconciliation between husband and wife with long discussions (and innumerable cups of tea) before the fugitive was finally admitted into the convent. Nevertheless, sanctuary was still offered up to the end of the Meiji era (1868–1912), when the community of nuns died out. The graveyard contains the tomb of the last abbess, and it bears the date 7 May 1902.

The temple grounds become very crowded at weekends (presumably owing to the place's divorce fame) and especially at the beginning of March when the plum blossoms offer a magnificent sight. Beyond the temple buildings stretches the very lovely and peaceful cemetery, set amid green bamboo and towering cryptomeria trees. Once more the visitor can appreciate the Japanese genius for harmonizing and blending man-made contructions with nature. No effort has been made to regiment nature in straight and orderly lines in the cramped valley. Instead the tombs are dispersed here and there in no discernible pattern according to the natural lay of the land. And what a beautiful site it is, especially in early December when the ground is thickly carpeted with bright yellow leaves.

In addition to the graves of local residents, the tombs of various distinguished people are to be found here. Up the double flight of stone steps to the right is a small plateau with the tombs of the abbesses of the convent. To the far right is a small cave containing the tomb of the foundress, the wife of Hōjō Tokimune; she established the convent in 1285 and became the first abbess. There is also the tomb of Princess Yōdō, the fifth abbess and the daughter of Emperor Go-Daigo (who, it will be remembered, successfully attacked Kamakura in 1333). The twentieth abbess, Tenshū, also has her tomb here. She was the granddaughter of the great Toyotomi Hideyoshi (one of the three unifiers of Japan in the sixteenth century) and the daughter of his ill-fated son, Hideyori. When Tokugawa troops stormed Osaka Castle in 1615, she managed to escape with her life, and it was probably in order to placate the victorious Tokugawa shogunate that she shaved her head and retired to Tōkei-ji. Richard Cocks heard something about this, and writing only a year after the fall of Osaka Castle, he noted: "The littell doughter of Hideyori Samma is shorne now in this monastery, only to save her life, for it is a sanctuary and no justis may take her out." Cocks does not seem to have received very flattering reports of the convent for he refers to the place as "a nunry (or rather a stews) of shaven women."

The graves of some celebrated modern figures can also be found to the left of the main path. Among these people may be mentioned Daisetz Suzuki, the philosophers Tetsurō Watsuji (d. 1960) and Kitarō Nishida (d. 1945), the publisher Shigeo Iwanami (d. 1946), the author Jun Takami (d. 1965), and the scholar and Education Minister Yoshishige Abe (d. 1966). They could hardly have chosen a more beautiful and peaceful resting place.

JŌCHI-JI   Just before you reach the level crossing, a turning to the right leads to the approaches of this small temple. It was founded in 1283 by Murotoki, Tokimune's grandson, and is still ranked as the fourth of the five great Zen temples of Kamakura. Fire and earthquake have taken their toll and little remains of its former splendor. But the surroundings are rather lovely and it is well worth a visit. You cross over a small stone bridge spanning a stream and climb up the worn steps into the temple precincts. The temple building on the right houses three statues that can barely be made out in the dim natural lighting—Amida, Shaka, and Miroku, representing past, present, and future. A monument of modern design, consisting of a sphere balanced on a pillar, bears the one word "Peace."

In recent years the temple has begun to charge for admittance into the precincts, and perhaps to justify this fee a further section of the garden has been opened to the public. The winding path is pleasant enough and passes in front of various tombs and caves; by walking around the grounds you can get some idea of the extent of the temple when it was an active, flourishing concern.

Jōchi-ji also has a well called Kanro no Ido (Nectar Well), and this is proudly represented as one of Kamakura's Ten Clear Wells. Kamakura has a penchant for numerical grouping of ancient monuments—Ten Clear Wells, Five Zen Temples, Ten Bridges, Five Springs, Seven Entrances, Twenty-Four Jizō, and Ten Amida, to mention just a few.

MEIGETSU-IN   On the other side of the level crossing a small road runs off to the left. A stream flows by the side of this road and most of the houses have to be approached by crossing over miniature bridges spanning the moat, bringing to mind Mr. Wemmick's cosy stronghold in *Great Expectations*. At the turn of the road, you reach Meigetsu-in, whose name can be romantically translated as the Temple of the Clear Moon.

The temple was founded under the auspices of Uesugi Norikata, whose tomb can be visited to the left of the entrance. A more prominent tomb, however, is that of Hōjō Tokiyori, the fifth Kamakura regent; he retired from office in 1256, became a monk with the name of Dōsō, and traveled incognito about the country to check administration abuses and help the ordinary people. An impoverished samurai who once burned his prize bonsai tree to provide warmth for his disguised visitor was later suitably rewarded.

The main temple building is new, but it is generally closed to visitors; nearby is an ancient thatched-roof shrine dedicated to the memory of the temple's founder. A recent innovation is a frame on which hang dozens of wooden *ema* votive tablets; on these are written the various petitions of the donors. Ema means horse picture, and although such tablets are usually decorated with pictures of horses, these at Meigetsu-in have paintings of hydrangeas, for reasons that will soon be apparent.

In the grounds of the temple is located one of Kamakura's biggest *yagura,* or burial caves, with dimly lit statues around the walls. This is an extremely interesting spot to explore, but access is not permitted to the casual visitor.

Located off the beaten track, Meigetsu-in usually enjoys a quiet and peaceful atmosphere; at times the only living being in evidence is a plump cat, lazily sunning itself on a balcony. But in June every year this idyllic scene is abruptly transformed as hundreds of sightseers converge on the spot; excursion buses edge gingerly along the crowded approach road, traffic jams form, policemen blow their whistles, portable toilets are installed, families proceed through the temple grounds, cameras click and flash. Why this sudden and not altogether happy change?

Then answer is simple—the hydrangea, or in Japanese, *ajisai*. If you like hydrangeas (I personally don't care for them and think that they are a rather coarse flower), then Meigetsu-in is the place for you in June. The garden becomes a mass of pink, blue, and white flowers, acres and acres of them. And this is what all the noise and bustle is about. It's certainly good that visitors can come and enjoy themselves in the garden admiring the flowers, and children can play in the open air amid the colorful hydrangeas. But it's also rather nice when the flowers fade, the crowds depart for another year, and the sleepy old cat can once more lazes undisturbed in the summer sun on the temple balcony.

KENCHŌ-JI   In marked contrast to the two smaller institutions just mentioned, Kenchō-ji invariably presents a picture of activity and prosperity. It is, in fact, the first of the Five Zen Temples of Kamakura and was founded in 1253 (that is, in the Kenchō era, 1249–55, and hence its name) under the patronage of the regent Hōjō Tokiyori. Its first abbot was a Chinese monk called Tao Lung (in Japanese, Dōryū), better known by his posthumous title, Daigaku Zenji.

Although the temple grounds are still extensive, in former times this Zen foundation must have covered a vast area if you can judge by old sketch maps depicting the numerous subtemples and buildings dotting the site. In recent times the size of its grounds has been further decreased by the construction of the school to the left of the main entrance.

The traditional wooden gate at the entrance bears a wooden

plaque featuring characters written in gold by Emperor Go-Fukakusa, who was reigning at the time of Kenchō-ji's foundation. The gate dates from 1783 and was transferred to this site as recently as 1943. A path lined by cherry trees leads into the precincts. In the first week of April this presents a rather fine sight, with the delicate colors of the fragile blossoms contrasted with the somber-hued, unpainted main gate in the background. Merry groups of visitors, not to say revelers, spread straw matting on the ground beneath the canopy of blossom and sit in amiable comradery, composing poetry and drinking sakè; and if poetic inspiration fails them, there is always the sakè to fall back on.

Possibly some Western observers might find it strange that such jovial gatherings are held in the grounds of a temple, and of an austere Zen monastery at that, but there seems to be no harm in people enjoying themselves in such fashion. William Blake would certainly have agreed on this point:

> But if at the Church they would give us some Ale,
> And a pleasant fire, our souls to regale:
> We'd sing and we'd pray all the live-long day:
> Nor ever once wish from the Church to stray.

Beyond the avenue of cherry trees stands one of the finest wooden structures in Kamakura, the great main gate through which the visitor passes to reach the complex of temple buildings beyond. This massive building has been designed with such skill and art that, despite its bulk and size, its graceful lines make it appear light and elegant. Examine the sturdy pillars and the intricate pattern of the eaves, and then marvel at the Japanese technical and artistic genius displayed in traditional construction. The gate was renovated in 1755, and its second floor houses statues of the 500 Rakan. But as in the case of Engaku-ji's gate, visitors are no longer allowed to climb upstairs.

To the right of the gate hangs Kamakura's second largest bell, almost two meters in height; made in 1255 by the master caster Shigemitsu Mononobe, it has been designated a National Treasure. Some time ago the temple authorities announced that, to preserve this valuable bell, outsiders would no longer be allowed to ring it on New Year's Eve; even more, the bell would be rung only eighteen, instead of the traditional 108, times. I am intrigued by the choice of eighteen. Does this number have, I wonder, some mystical significance, or was it obtained by merely reversing the first two digits of 108? Nobody seems to know.

To the left of the belfry a path flanked by tall cryptomerias runs up the hillside and leads to the monks' quarters, behind which a long flight of steps forms an impressive approach to the tomb of the temple's founder. But this part of the precincts is strictly off limits to the ordinary visitor and so need not be described.

Just beyond the main gate, to the left of the path, grows (or perhaps just exists) an old juniper tree. Its gnarled and writhing boughs, propped up in their extremely old age by wooden crutches, meander this way and that. The juniper is said to have been planted by Kenchō-ji's first abbot; this would make it more than 700 years old and, as regards longevity, a competitor to the gingko in Hachiman Shrine.

The first of the two main buildings is called the Buddha Hall, and it was brought to the present site in 1647 (traditionally built Japanese buildings can be relatively easily dismantled and reassembled). Inside the hall is a large seated statue of Jizō, and within this image is supposed to be a miniature statue of Jizō that once saved a man's life. Kenchō-ji is located on an old execution site, and before being led to his fate, a condemned man once hid this little image of Jizō in his topknot. As a result of this pious subterfuge, the executioner, try as he might, was unable to cut off his head, and the man was set free. On ceremonial occasions the brightly robed monks can be seen gathered in this hall reciting sutras. This is one aspect of monastic life that is seldom elaborated in English-language books on Zen.

The second building is called the Hōdō, or Hall of the Law, and was rebuilt in 1814. This is mainly used for zazen. You can sometimes see rows of lay people seated on cushions, their legs crossed in front of them in the lotus position (or in the semilotus position, if they cannot manage the full one), and a sentinel monk silently and measuredly pacing up and down between the rows with his wooden staff held aloft, ready to beat with a resounding *thwack!* the shoulder of any practitioner suspected of dozing during the session. There is a good deal of Zen lay activity held in both Kenchō-ji and Engaku-ji, and notice boards announce the times of the regular zazen sessions.

The last of the main buildings is enclosed within a courtyard and is called the Ryūōden, or Hall of the Dragon King. As may be seen by the lines of its ornamental roof, the gateway in front of this building is Chinese in style and would appear to date from early in the Edo period (1603–1868). Visitors are allowed to walk around the balcony skirting the Ryūōden and can admire the pond and garden behind the building. Unlike Kyoto, with its wealth of magnificent gardens, Kamakura has few on public display, and this is probably the best of its kind. The garden is supposed to have been laid out by the monk Musō Kokushi, who died in 1351, and the shape of the pond represents the Chinese character 心 meaning heart or mind; or so we are told, for it takes some imagination to be able to discern this symbolism. But it takes little imagination to appreciate the beauty of this small garden and the subtle way in which the wooded hills in the background have been incorporated into the overall design.

The main path continues to the left of the Ryūōden. Various smaller sloping paths lead off to subtemples and a cemetery; the artistically decrepit steps are shaded by maple trees and present a colorful sight in late autumn. The main path turns a sharp right and leads off to Hansōbō and Ten'en Park, but these will be dealt with in a later chapter. If instead of taking this right turn visitors carry straight on and walk up the shallow steps flanked by a small statue of a Chinese sage, they will reach one of the most charming subtemples in Kenchō-ji, or, for that matter, in the whole of Kamakura. The precincts appear to be semiprivate, but there seems to be no objection to anybody making a quiet and respectful visit. The temple was formerly located in Jōchi-ji and was subsequently transferred to this quiet setting. The peaceful garden is a delight to see in late autumn. It contains statues of the Six Jizō in a grotto and various old tombs, one of them being that of a son of Emperor Go-Saga. Go-Saga ascended the throne in 1243 thanks to the influence of the Hōjō family, and so he was always beholden to the Kamakura administration. He reigned as emperor only three years, but, as in the case of other ex-emperors, as abdicated emperor he continued to wield power for twenty-six more years until he died in 1272.

ENNŌ-JI   This interesting Zen foundation was established by the monk Chikaku, but was located in various different places in Kamakura until it was transferred to the present site in 1702 after it had been destroyed by an earthquake and tidal wave in the previous year. Its chief and perhaps only claim to fame is its collection of ferocious statues representing the judges of hell who weigh sinners in the balance after their deaths.

The statues are set around the three sides of a small hall, with King Emma occupying the principal place in the center; his statue is in fact appreciably larger than those of his fellow judges. The expression on his face is far from benign and is enough to strike terror in anybody's heart. Lafcadio Hearn speaks of it as "tremendous, menacing, frightful," and for once I am prepared to agree with his assessment. To the left are seated five of his crowned attendants—Taizan, Toshi, Godō Keirin, Hyōtō, and Gokan— while on the right-hand side glower Sōtei, Shinkō, and Henjō. Emma should be surrounded by nine attendants, but Shōkō has been removed from the temple and may be conveniently seen in the Kokuhōkan in the grounds of Hachiman Shrine. The positioning of the statues around the walls would seem to indicate that the sinner is summoned to appear before the judges seated in plenary session, but this is not so; the wretched person has to meet each of the scowling judges one by one, and then finally receive sentence from Emma himself.

The horrendous depiction of Emma has inevitably given rise to a host of legends and tales. According to one, the celebrated sculptor Unkei died and duly appeared before Emma. The judge angrily asked him why he had never made a statue of the King of Hell. Unkei replied that as he had never before seen Emma's countenance, he had been unable to make the statue—a somewhat lame excuse, for Unkei had made plenty of statues of other unseen deities. Whereupon the irate judge sent Unkei back to earth to remedy this defect. After the commission had been duly accomplished, the sculptor returned once more to the next life where, one may hope, he met a mollified Emma. Yet another man was sent back to this world by Emma because he had arrived earlier than scheduled, and he was guided from the nether world to Kamakura by the sound of the bell in Engaku-ji. And Emma pardoned a poor woman condemned to the pains of the deepest hell because in her kindness she had once placed a cap on the head of the Jizō statue in Kenchō-ji to keep it warm in cold weather.

To the right of the entrance door of the hall are two statues that, although sitting in line with the judges, do not belong to Emma's court. The one nearest the door depicts the seated Zen monk Chikaku, the founder of the temple; this is a fine representative example of the realistic portrayal of Zen monks, warts and all (yet another example of this type of statue is the figure of Musō Kokushi in Zuisen-ji). In contrast, the next statue is that of Datsueba, which literally means Robe-Stealing Hag. The name succinctly sums up the occupation of this disagreeable character, for she seizes the robes of people as they pass into the nether world. Poor souls, as if they had not got enough to worry about without her adding to their troubles.

Northeastern Kamakura

Kamakura ──*20 min.*──▶ Harakiri Cave ──*15 min.*──▶
Station   腹切やぐら

Shakadō Tunnel ──*15 min.*──▶ Egara Tenjin ──*10 min.*──▶
釈迦堂切通し   荏柄天神

Yoritomo's Tomb ──*10 min.*──▶ Kamakura Shrine ──*25 min.*──▶
頼朝の墓   鎌倉宮

Zuisen-ji ──*40 min.*──▶ Kakuon-ji
瑞泉寺   覚園寺

THIS PART OF THE CITY, that is, to the right and rear of Hachiman Shrine, is full of historical interest, for this was the area where the administrative offices of the Kamakura government were housed and consequently many high-ranking officials had their mansions. Admittedly the first two places listed below fall a little bit outside this area, but they are included here for the sake of convenience, as visitors can take them in while walking from the station.

HARAKIRI CAVE   The approach to this site runs along a quiet narrowing country lane and passes over Kamakura's one and only river, the Namerigawa (Nameri River). The name literally means Smooth River or Gliding River and is apt enough; unlike the great rivers of Tokyo, Osaka, and Kyoto, the water never seems to be in a hurry to get anywhere and just meanders along at a tranquil rate. Often no wider than a stream, this river could never have been used for transportation purposes; in fact, it is very shallow along its entire route and barely measures six kilometers from its source in eastern Kamakura to Yuigahama beach, where it trickles out into the sea.

Now that I have mentioned this river, it is inevitable that a celebrated story concerning it has to be told. The Hōjō regents Tokiyori and Tokimune were fortunate enough to have an official called Aoto Fujitsuna serving them. Famous for both his integrity and wisdom, Aoto once accidently dropped a few copper coins into the Namerigawa; he immediately ordered an exhaustive search for the money and was not satisfied until every single coin had been recovered. This caused a certain amount of local criticism because the operation had cost far more than the few lost coins were worth. But Aoto instantly silenced his economy-minded critics by pointing out that the outlay of public funds had been beneficial as it had put money into the pockets of the men fishing around for the coins in the river.

One can't help feeling that there was some flaw in his argument, but the episode made Aoto famous and earned for him a niche in Japanese folklore. And "folklore" is perhaps the best word to use in this context, because historians are not at all convinced that Aoto ever existed and suspect that this righteous official may have been invented as an example for others to follow.

At any rate, the bridge over the Namerigawa affords a pleasant enough view of the stream; it is a quiet and peaceful spot, and trees on both banks lean over the water, forming in summer a cool, green tunnel. But the place was not always so quiet and peaceful, and the name of the bridge, Tōshō-ji Bridge, brings to mind tumultuous events that took place here more than six hundred years ago.

Tōshō-ji temple no longer exists, but it was probably located beyond the bridge on the left-hand side of the road. This Zen temple was founded by Hōjō Yasutoki in 1237 to hold memorial services for his mother, who was buried in the locality. It was destroyed during the fifteenth century and then restored in the early part of the following century, only to be demolished once more at some unknown date. But its fame rests on the fact that it was here that the last Hōjō regent, Takatoki, decided to commit suicide in 1333 when no further resistance could be offered against the imperial army attacking the city.

It was, in a way, an ironic decision to choose this particular temple, for Tōshō-ji literally means Eastern Victory Temple, and the fall of Kamakura signaled the complete destruction of the eastern forces, the Hōjō regents and the Kamakura shogunate. But the spot had been the burial ground for many of Takatoki's ancestors, and it was probably this consideration that made the young regent take refuge in the temple.

The fourteenth-century warrior story *Taiheiki* (an ironic title, for it can be translated as Record of the Great Peace) describes in lyrical detail the mighty acts of heroism and valor performed by the Hōjō forces in their desperate defense of the city. Realizing that the situation was hopeless, a messenger hurried to the temple to advise the people there that all was lost and that they should do away with themselves. Whereupon many of the officers and courtiers committed ritual suicide by cutting their stomachs.

One of the officers delayed killing himself because he was afraid that Takatoki might lose his nerve and disgrace the Hōjō family by not committing suicide honorably. But spurred on by the example of a fifteen-year-old boy who fearlessly performed the agonizing rite in front of him, Takatoki took up his dagger and died bravely.

Some 870 persons likewise killed themselves in this place, and the bodies of many of them were consumed by the flames that later swept through the temple. Certainly 10 July 1333 must have been a day of unmitigated horror in this small valley. Not that visitors today could have any notion of this dreadful slaughter as they walk up the quiet and peaceful lane. All that there is to be seen at the end of the valley is a large monument recounting past events and the small Harakiri Cave where Takatoki is supposed to have ended his life. But memories are long in Kamakura, and even today it is not rare to find fresh flowers and burning incense in the cave. Close nearby is a Catholic retreat house, and people attending sessions there in this historical spot doubtless find it easy to meditate on the ephemeral glory of this world.

SHAKADŌ TUNNEL   As I mentioned in the first chapter, Kamakura's hilly terrain added immense strategic value to the city in time of attack. But the surrounding hills jut into the main valley, thus forming a complex of smaller valleys within the city itself. This presented a considerable inconvenience to local people wanting to get from one place to another, for they either had to walk over or around the intervening hills—or through them. Hence Kamakura has quite a number of handy tunnels enabling the residents of one small valley to pass easily into the next. One of the longer ones, in fact, the Sannōgayatsu Tunnel, is passed through on the way from the Harakiri Cave to the Shakadō Tunnel.

The name Shakadō means Buddha Hall, and Yasutoki, whose devotion to his departed mother has just been mentioned, also built in this vicinity in 1225 a temple in which services were to be held for his father, Yoshitoki, who had been assassinated in the previous year. The chief object of veneration at this temple was a statue of Shaka, the historical Buddha, and hence arose the name of this area. The temple no longer exists; the statue is said to have been transferred to nearby Sugimoto-ji and later to a temple in Meguro, Tokyo. Hōjō Tokimasa certainly had a mansion on the south side (that is, toward the city) of the Shakadō Tunnel, and thus the tunnel may have been constructed as an escape exit in case of a surprise attack.

Whatever its original purpose, this high-roofed tunnel has long served as a convenient passage for people walking from the shopping area in central Kamakura to the northeastern districts of

Shakadō Tunnel, dating from the thirteenth century.

the city. In recent years this ancient tunnel has been officially closed because of the danger of falling rocks, and motor traffic no longer passes through. But centuries-old traditions die hard in Kamakura, and people still walk through this cavernous passage. For, more than a tunnel, it seems to resemble a large and lofty cave running through the line of hills. I wonder whether it is an entirely man-made construction, for it was hardly necessary to have made the roof so high that a double-decker bus could pass through.

Burial caves can be seen high up in the walls of the tunnel, but many more exist unseen on the hill above. Kamakura has literally hundreds of these caves, located, often enough, in rather inaccessible places in the hills. The local rock tends to be fairly soft, and so it was relatively simple to dig out caves (or enlarge existing natural ones) as burial places and thus preserve the limited amount of flat land for residential purposes.

There are about fifty caves (some of them amounting to no more than shallow niches in the rock) above the Shakadō Tunnel. The best-preserved burial caves in Kamakura have low entrances, obliging visitors to stoop as they enter. These entrances lead into square, flat-roofed chambers. Generally there are remains of statues and tombstones in evidence, as well as niches in the walls or holes in the floor in which the ashes of the person to be buried were deposited. Here above the Shakadō Tunnel were found large quantities of charred human bones early in the present century, together with bits and pieces of swords and other weapons. For a long time it was thought that the warriors who were killed or committed suicide in the 1333 defense of the city were brought here from Tōshō-ji for burial. But it was only in 1965, after a minor landslide uncovered various historical relics, that a tombstone bearing the date 10 July 1333, the very day that Kamakura fell, was found, thus showing that the legend was based on historical fact.

The caves above the tunnel also served as damp and chilly prisons. One is called Karaito Cave and was used to confine a woman of that name, the daughter of Tezuka Mitsumori. Mitsumori was a retainer of Minamoto Yoshinaka (often called Kiso Yoshinaka, after his birthplace), a relative of Yoritomo; despite their relationship, Mitsumori fell out with Yoritomo and was eventually killed in battle in 1184. Before this, however, he had instructed Karaito to slip into Kamakura and spy on Yoritomo. Karaito did so, but was discovered and locked up in this dank cave.

Whereupon her daughter, Manju-hime, traveled to Kamakura and, without revealing her identity, entered Yoritomo's service. At a New Year's banquet she sang so beautifully that Yoritomo promised to grant any wish she might care to make. The twelve-year-old girl confessed her identity and begged to be allowed to take her mother's place in prison. The story has a happy ending (unusual in those cruel days), for the general was so moved by Manju's filial devotion that he released Karaito and sent both mother and daughter back home.

EGARA TENJIN This is an old Shinto shrine, founded in 1104 and dedicated to Tenjin, the patron deity of scholarship. Before his deification, Tenjin was Sugawara Michizane, a government minister serving the emperors Uda and Daigo in the ninth century. He strove to strengthen the authority of the throne and thus incurred the enmity of court families such as the Fujiwara, who in their own interests were trying to weaken the political power of the emperor. Believing the calumnies made against his minister, Daigo exiled him to Kyushu in 901, where he died two years later.

Despite this shabby treatment, Michizane's loyalty toward the throne never wavered. One of the few pleasures left to him in Kyushu was to climb to the summit of Mount Tempai, face the direction of Kyoto, and bow in veneration to the emperor. Another consolation was his plum tree. Michizane was very fond of plum blossoms, and at the time of his banishment his favorite plum tree reportedly uprooted itself and flew off to join him in exile, thus earning for itself the name Tobi-ume, or Flying Plum Tree.

After Michizane's death, a series of natural calamities—storms, floods, and earthquakes—showed clearly enough that divine displeasure had been aroused at the unjust treatment of the loyal minister. So the late Michizane was given increasingly higher posthumous ranks to appease his troubled spirit. In the course of time he came to be regarded as a deity, and from 959 he has been venerated at the famous Kitano Shrine in Kyoto. He was a learned man and a noted poet, so it is only natural that he should be considered the patron of scholarship. He is also regarded as the patron deity of literature, and on 25 January every year discarded *fude,* or writing brushes, together with some lowly ball pens, are solemnly burned at this shrine in Kamakura.

The shrine is approached through the usual torii gateway, with two old nettle trees leaning over at a crazy angle to form a second, natural archway. At the top of the flight of steps is a large gingko tree that is said to be more than 900 years old. The shrine buildings themselves are not outstanding, but the votive ema tablets to be seen in their hundreds to the right are interesting. Because of Michizane's fondness for plum blossoms, these ex-votos show a seated figure with plum blossoms in the background, rather than the usual picture of a horse.

As Michizane is the patron of scholarship, his popularity has boomed in recent years in the mad rush to pass entrance examinations and enter prestigious universities. Thus all these tablets carry petitions for success in the annual "examination hell" that takes place in spring. But a vaguely worded prayer would not appear to be enough. Instead the young clients carefully list not only the universities but even the very departments that they hope to enter. As a sort of insurance, most hopefuls will take the entrance examinations for two or three universities in the hope of being accepted by at least one.

For one particular student to write down the names of three universities on the tablet would not seem to indicate a great deal of faith in Michizane's efficacy. But Michizane had a lot to suffer in his lifetime, and he probably feels deep sympathy for the young people forced to take part in such an inhuman system. I noticed recently that one boy had listed no fewer than *ten* universities. Whether this was just wishful thinking on his part, I don't know, but it is incredible that he should have taken the examinations of so many institutions of higher learning in one year. "May I finally receive the crown of learning," he wrote lyrically on the tablet. Well, I hope at least he managed to enter a university, with or without the desired crown.

YORITOMO'S TOMB   One would have thought that Yoritomo, the founder of the Kamakura administration and the man who put the city on the map, so to speak, would be duly honored by the grateful inhabitants with a splendid tomb. After all, if he had set up his headquarters elsewhere in 1180, there would have been no Kamakura period in Japanese history and art; neither would the Daibutsu (Great Buddha) have been constructed, nor would the great Zen temples have been founded here.

Perhaps the achievements of such men in their own lifetimes are their best memorial, and they hardly need pretentious monuments to keep their memory fresh. Whatever the reason, there can be no denying that Yoritomo's tomb is a decidedly unworthy memorial for the founder of the city; in fact, plenty of lesser men, about whom we know very little, have been honored with far more impressive tombs elsewhere in Kamakura. The approach to Yoritomo's tomb is promising enough; the way is lined with cherry trees and steps lead up to a small plateau in the hillside. But the tomb itself, enclosed within a stone fence, is an uninscribed and insignificant affair, although its natural setting, with a tall tree towering protectively over it, is rather pleasant.

Yoritomo was an able and conscientious administrator, and the famous portrait at Jingo-ji in Kyoto depicting him in court robes shows us a strong, shrewd personality. It was perhaps in keeping with his character that his death was caused by an accident suffered while performing his official duties. He had been out to inaugurate a new bridge on the last day of 1198, and while he was returning he fell from his horse; he died six weeks later at the age of 52. Had he lived a few years longer, he would have had time to settle the problem of succession and much of the subsequent bloodshed might have been avoided. His tomb is located in the Nikaidō district, and this was the area where many of the government offices were situated and where, it is believed, he himself lived.

A rather steep path leads off from the right of his tomb to the resting place of two men closely associated with him, but it is advisable to go down the steps and walk along the alley to reach these tombs. They are set high up on the hillside at the top of a double flight of 153 steps, and the sight of this ascent is enough to dismay the hearts of all but the most determined visitors. At the top there are two caves containing the tombs of Ōe Hiromoto, who served Yoritomo from the very earliest days and helped to organize his government administration, and Shimazu Tadahisa, an illegitimate son of Yoritomo.

Tadahisa's mother wisely fled to Kyushu to escape the wrath of Yoritomo's wife, Masako, and her son eventually became the governor of Satsuma Province. In 1196 he built a castle in a place called Shimazu, took this name for himself, and thus founded the illustrious Shimazu family.

And so here on the quiet hillside rest three men who enjoyed power and authority in their lifetimes. What does it matter if their monuments are something less than impressive? The trio's achievements speak for themselves.

KAMAKURA SHRINE   Of Kamakura's sixty-five temples and nineteen shrines, this is one of the two foundations of modern origin—and by modern I mean that it is barely more than a hundred years old. This span of time may appear long by some standards, yet when compared to the 1,200-year history of nearby Sugimoto-ji, it is just a passing moment. Yet the shrine occupies a historical site and commemorates an event that took place back in 1335, exactly two years after the fall of Kamakura.

It will be remembered that in 1333 Emperor Go-Daigo took advantage of the faltering authority of the Kamakura government, rallied dissident generals to the imperial cause, and took the city by storm. On the fall of the Hōjō family, political power was restored to the old capital of Kyoto, but in the ensuing intrigue Go-Daigo enjoyed supreme authority for only a brief time before the Ashikaga family replaced the Hōjōs as the virtual rulers of Japan.

Prince Morinaga was Go-Daigo's third son and was outstanding in his devotion to the imperial cause. Before the fall of the Kamakura shogunate, the Hōjō regent prevented his becoming crown prince, so Morinaga became a monk and retired to the monastery on Mount Hiei. On the fall of the Hōjō government, Morinaga came out of his monastic retirement, was appointed shogun, and resumed his championing the rights of the throne. This did not suit the purposes of the emerging Ashikaga family, and it was decided that it would be expedient to get the young man out of the way, thus weakening the emperor's power. So, just like Sugawara Michizane four hundred years earlier, Morinaga was denounced to the throne as a scheming traitor and imprisoned in a small cave to the rear of the present Kamakura Shrine. In 1335, after being cooped up in the narrow cell for several months, the 27-year-old Morinaga was led out and beheaded. Only too late did his father, Go-Daigo, realize that his son had been maligned and was innocent of the charges of treason.

In 1868 the Imperial Restoration took place, and power was returned to civilian hands for the first time since Yoritomo became shogun in 1192. After so many centuries of shogunal rule, most commoners had only the vaguest idea of the rightful role of the throne. For hundreds of years the emperors had been residing obscure and unseen in Kyoto while the shoguns wielded all the real power, and it must have been bewildering for ordinary people to suddenly find that they had a new type of ruler. So a public-relations campaign was launched by the new government to introduce the young Emperor Meiji and to explain the newly restored imperial authority. What better way to instill loyalty to the throne into Japanese citizens than by reviving and revering the memory of the loyalist Prince Michinaga? So an imperial order was issued by the seventeen-year-old emperor in 1869, only a few months after the shogunal government had handed back administrative power to him, commanding that a shrine be founded in Kamakura to venerate the memory of Morinaga. The emperor's advisers wasted no time in establishing this monument to imperial loyalty in Kamakura, probably because the place had always been associated with military, non-imperial government. While the founding of this shrine was symbolic, it certainly had political overtones. After the construction of the buildings and precincts were completed, Emperor Meiji came to visit the place in 1873, and various mementos of this occasion are still on display.

The shrine stands on the site of an old Zen temple called Tōkō-ji, founded about the beginning of the thirteenth century, and it was in this temple that Morinaga was imprisoned. There is no record of when Tōkō-ji was destroyed, and its only link that remains with the present is the cave in which the unfortunate prince was kept prisoner. On payment of a fee, visitors are allowed to walk behind the main shrine building, view the outside of the barred cave, and inspect some of the objects commemorating Emperor Meiji's visit. On the whole this short tour holds little of interest for the ordinary visitor and can be safely omitted without much loss.

As for Morinaga, the young man is not, of course, buried within the precincts of the Shinto shrine. Instead his tomb is to be found about two kilometers to the northeast on top of a hill called Richikō-zan (this name is derived from an old temple of that name, Richikō-ji, or Temple of the Glory of Reason and Wisdom, that was on this site until 1868). The tomb itself is not very impressive, but its natural setting can be compared to some of the fine monuments of Kyoto and Nara in grandeur and size. A long flight of 168 stone steps runs straight up the hillside amid the tall cryptomeria trees. This must be one of the grandest sights of Kamakura, but as the place is off the beaten track, few people ever seem to find their way here.

Kamakura Shrine is not of great interest, although there is plenty of colorful activity to be seen at New Year's, the annual festival on 20 August (the date on which Morinaga was killed), and the children's 7-5-3 festival in October; it is also a very popular place for weddings.

There is, however, one annual event of absorbing interest: the *Takigi Nō,* the Noh performance that takes place by torchlight on the evening of 22 September. This type of performance is also staged elsewhere in Japan, at Kōfuku-ji in Nara, for example, and the custom began in Kamakura as recently as 1959. This is an extraordinarily moving experience, for the ancient Noh plays are performed in the open by the light of fires, just as they used to be before the invention of modern means of illumination. The open-air setting certainly contributes to the spectacle, but above all it is the weird effect that the flickering firelight has on the actors' masks that causes the occasion to be so memorable. The uneven lighting makes the masks come to life in a peculiarly vivid fashion, animating the wooden features in a way that is not seen in the steady glare of electric light in modern theaters.

The only problem is that demand for tickets for this performance far exceeds the number of places available. Applications for seats are chosen by lot, and so it is a chancy matter whether or not you can attend in any one particular year. But it is worth making the attempt and, who knows, you may be fortunate (I was lucky on my first try). If you are, you will participate in a truly moving and unforgettable experience.

ZUISEN-JI Of Kamakura's many temples, it is difficult to decide which one enjoys the most pleasant setting. But many people, if asked to choose, would probably mention Zuisen-ji, an old Zen foundation located on a secluded hillside with a fine view toward the sea.

Zuisen-ji was founded by the monk Musō Kokushi in 1327. So the temple began its existence only six years before the downfall of the Hōjō rulers, but it was fortunate enough to attract the patronage of the succeeding Ashikaga leaders, especially Takauji, the first shogun from that family. As a result, the temple flourished and was quite large in size, but all the buildings existing now are comparatively modern. As for its founder, Musō Kokushi was a learned monk who left behind treatises on Zen thought that are still studied today; he was also an accomplished calligrapher, poet, and political adviser.

One of the buildings at Zuisen-ji, in its beautiful natural surroundings.

The temple possesses a superb statue of this remarkable man, but unfortunately it is not shown to the general public without prior application. The seated wooden figure is about eighty centimeters in height and is locked away in a small shrine in the temple grounds. The statue was probably carved shortly after Musō's death in 1351, and the realistic depiction of both his face and robes is very striking. His calm, delicate features bear something of a quizzical look as he stares impassively ahead.

Musō is said to have practiced zazen in the three-apartment cave to the right of the formal rock-and-sand garden behind the main building. One of the caves has a hole in the wall, and this serves as a natural window with a pleasant view of the nearby green bamboo. The formal garden consists of rock, sand, and water, and was laid out by Musō himself (he also planned the principal garden of

Kenchō-ji; see page 34). Time was when the casual visitor was allowed to pass through this austere garden, inspect the caves, and climb up the steps cut into the cliff face behind; this flight of steps is known as the Jūhachi-mawari, or Eighteen Bends, because of its twists and turns, and it leads into Ten'en Park behind. But ordinary visitors are no longer allowed to enter Musō's cave and garden, or to climb up the cliff steps.

Formerly a small waterfall tumbled down the side of the cliff and splashed into the garden. Perhaps it originated from a spring in the hills above, because Zuisen-ji's name literally means Temple of the Abundant Spring. But alas, the spring is no longer abundant and the water no longer falls. But all is not lost, for I once had the privilege and pleasure of taking part in a tour of the temple conducted by the resident monk, and when we entered the famous garden he sent an employee up the hillside to turn on the (presumably artificial) water supply. And so once more we could admire and photograph the waterfall at will until the order was given to close the tap and the cascade dribbled to a halt. I'm not quite sure what Musō would have to say about this arrangement, but he would probably offer no objections. After all, although traditional Japanese gardens *look* so very natural, a good deal of artifice is put into their making and upkeep.

Apart from the garden of sand, rocks, and (occasional) waterfall, the temple grounds can boast of a profusion of trees, shrubs, and plants, albeit some of the paths are laid out in rather geometric, straight lines unusual for a temple garden. This is an ideal place for casual strolling, and the precincts are crowded every March by people coming to view the splendid plum blossoms. And there is one year-round attraction—roosters strut around the garden, condescendingly pecking at the food offered by visitors and from time to time letting out a raucous cockadoodle-dooooo. This is a unique feature for a Kamakura temple and one which Musō would have heartily approved of, I suspect.

Otherwise there is not a great deal to be said about Zuisen-ji—

the place is more to be visited than described. I suppose one may make mention of Yoshida Shōin, a devoted loyalist who lived here for a short while. He tried to slip aboard one of Commodore Perry's ships in 1854 so that he could travel to the West, but he was discovered and returned ashore. He was jailed for this offense, but after his release he worked indefatigably for the restoration of the emperor's rights. Unfortunately for Yoshida, the time was not yet ripe for the imperial restoration, and the twenty-eight-year-old man was arrested and executed by the Tokugawa authorities.

But although Zuisen-ji may not have a very interesting history or possess readily accessible art treasures, it is an attractive spot and well worth a visit on a fine day.

KAKUON-JI   If many people would opt for Zuisen-ji as the most attractive temple complex in Kamakura, quite a few others would choose Kakuon-ji. Both are beautiful places, but the two differ completely as regards atmosphere and mood. Zuisen-ji gives you the impression of being fresh, light, welcoming, and happy; Kakuon-ji, on the other hand, is silent, withdrawn, contemplative, and remote. To some extent Kakuon-ji's atmosphere is due to its location off the beaten track, and its out-of-the-way site lends itself to a feeling of aloofness and privacy. No greater contrast could be found than between Kamakura Shrine and this temple. The former place is always bustling with visitors, tourists, and wedding guests; children feed the caged deer, their parents eat lunch at the large restaurant within the precincts, commemorative photos of tour groups are taken.

Kakuon-ji is not so very far away, and yet it seems a world apart. All is silent, all is peaceful: no shops, no vending machines, no tour groups, no photographs allowed. It is very often quite difficult to enter the grounds at all. When a disparate group of half-a-dozen people have assembled at the gate, a guide (often a monk) may or may not emerge, sometimes with seeming reluctance, to show the intruders around. Thumbing his rosary, he leads the group around a limited part of the grounds. Visitors are sternly admonished not to take photos, and stragglers are firmly exhorted to join the flock and not dawdle off by themselves. Only three places are shown, and then brief explanations, including some words of religious exhortation, are given tersely and to the point.

Kakuon-ji began its existence in 1218 when Hōjō Yoshitoki built a Buddha Hall on this site, but it was not until 1296 that it was upgraded to the full status of a temple. Its first abbot was a monk called Chikai Shin'e, about whom not a great deal is known. After the fall of the Hōjō family, the temple was patronized by the succeeding Ashikaga administration and even by Emperor Go-Daigo. It was damaged by fire, but with the help of Ashikaga Takauji, the Buddha Hall was restored in 1354. Kakuon-ji appears to have been a teaching center of Buddhist doctrine, expounding the tenets of the Shingon, Zen, and Jōdo sects; this eclectic approach was abandoned at the beginning of the Meiji era, and the temple is now viewed as belonging to the esoteric Shingon school.

The guide leads visitors slowly through the temple's extensive grounds and finally reaches an old thatched-roof Buddha Hall, the building restored in 1354. Here the main door is solemnly unpadlocked and the group is invited to enter. And what a surprise awaits anybody visiting the place for the first time. The small dim hall is dominated by three large statues seated on lotus thrones upon the sanctuary. In the center sits the figure of Yakushi Nyorai, the Healing Buddha, who has vowed to cure all diseases and is also venerated as the deity of longevity. He is flanked on either side by somewhat smaller statues of his attendants, Nikkō and Gakkō Bosatsu, representing the sun and moon deities respectively. Each of the three statues is framed by its *funa-gokō,* the large halolike decoration creating a background for the entire body. Traces of the original bright coloring are still plainly visible, but centuries of incense smoke and quiet neglect have dimmed the statues' former brilliance.

These are superb creations, and the fact that they are housed (or rather venerated, for the monk will reverently light incense in front of them) in this old remote hall, with its clay floor and dim, natural lighting, only serves to enhance their ethereal beauty. For this is the sort of setting in which their sculptors meant them to be seen—not in the clinical atmosphere of a museum or under bright lights or subjected to the indignity of flash photographs and the rude gaze of noisy tourists, but seated calmly and majestically in the religious atmosphere of a timeworn rustic temple.

The two side walls of the hall are lined with a dozen tall statues of standing warrior deities, their swirling robes, menacing spears and swords, and glaring glass eyes forming a startling contrast to the serene triad seated on the sanctuary. The ceiling has a painting of a dragon, but the bright coloring has largely faded, and the dim lighting makes it difficult to see the details clearly.

The visiting group is allowed only five or six minutes inside the Buddha Hall and is then politely ushered out. The monk carefully padlocks the door once more, and the figures within return again to their time-long darkness and silence. Two large burial caves are visited, and then the party reaches a small Jizō shrine. To the left is a row of six bibbed and capped Jizō statues (you will often find these statues in lines of half a dozen; there is one such group on an old execution site on the main road between Wakamiya Avenue and Hase), but the shrine is renowned not for the six figures outside but for the large one within.

This is the Black Jizō, thus called on account of its unusual dusky color; however often in the past it has been painted a brighter and more cheerful color, it has invariably returned to its dark appearance by the following day. Some assert that it is because this Jizō braves the flames of hell to rescue sinners condemned to punishment there. Whether this is true or not, the statue has become fittingly enough the patron of local firemen and attracts considerable numbers of devotees at its annual festival on 10 August.

That is the end of the brief conducted tour. All that visitors see is the Buddha Hall, the burial caves, and the Black Jizō. And the garden, of course. The secluded surroundings are extraordinarily beautiful and peaceful; old trees and fresh bamboo grow in abundance, birds sing, water flows. The garden, completely carpeted with yellow leaves, is a magnificent sight in late autumn. The place is also attractive in spring, but somehow or other the mellow and somewhat melancholy season of autumn seems to fit in best with Kakuon-ji's remote and somewhat mysterious atmosphere.

There are various other places of interest in the grounds, and I well remember visiting them years ago. There is one of Kamakura's famous ten wells, said to have been dug by Kōbō Daishi, the founder of the Shingon sect of Buddhism, and, indeed, a benign, seated statue of this ninth-century priest is located close by. There is, or was, a path leading up into Ten'en Park at the rear of the precincts. There are some splendid tombs, including those of the first two abbots. There are a number of interesting burial caves in addition to the two shown on the guided tour. There is the tomb of the well-known historical novelist Shōfū Muramatsu (d. 1961).

However, none of these places is any longer accessible, although I suppose that, with the right introduction and patient prior negotiations, it might be possible to visit them. But I for one cannot resent this guarding of privacy against tourist intrusion. We can only be grateful that a small tantalizing glimpse of Kakuon-ji's beautiful interior is allowed at all.

Eastern Environs

Kamakura Station	30 min. Bus: 15 min.	→	Sugimoto-ji 杉本寺	10 min.	→
	Hōkoku-ji 報国寺	10 min. →	Jōmyō-ji 浄妙寺	15min.	→
Kōsoku-ji 光触寺	15 min. →	Jūniso Shrine 十二所神社	20 min. →	Asahina Pass 朝比奈切通し	

THIS IS THE ROAD that runs out through the eastern part of the city, and if its meandering, tortuous route is any proof of antiquity, it must be an extremely old road. And if its antiquity were in doubt, there are records that show that this route served as one of the principal thoroughfares into and out of Kamakura seven centuries ago. The temples along the way are very different from the grand monastic establishments to be found in Kita-Kamakura, the other side of town, but they have a certain charm of their own, and each in its own fashion has something of interest for the visitor.

SUGIMOTO-JI   This fine old temple is reputed to be the oldest institution in the whole of Kamakura, for it was founded in 734 by order of Empress Kōmei, so it was well over four centuries old when Yoritomo marched his troops into the city and set up his military headquarters here. Built on the side of a hill, Sugimoto-ji

(The Temple at the Foot of the Cryptomeria) is approached by two flights of worn steps. Halfway up is a gateway from which two grimacing Niō statues scowl down fiercely at passersby.

They are not the biggest temple-guardians in Kamakura, for those in Hongaku-ji, for example, are larger. But they are undoubtedly the finest examples of their kind to be found within the city. Of course, they cannot compare with the pair of Niō statues towering eight meters high in front of Tōdai-ji in Nara, but they are well worth close inspection. The custom of placing guardian deities at temple gates to keep out unwelcome evil spirits goes back to India, and the statues represent the two Dêva kings, Indra and Brahma.

In Japan, they go by the names of Naraen-kongō (on the left) and Misshaku-kongō (on the right). The figure on the right normally has his mouth open, while his companion on the other side keep his firmly closed; you will notice the same is generally true of statues of foxes (*inari*) and lion-dogs in temples and shrines. One theory has it that the figure on the right is exclaiming the mystical syllable "A," while the other is mumbling "Um," the two being the alpha and omega of all existence. According to another theory, the figures represent two different aspects of one and the same being.

The muscled figure on the left normally has his hands empty, but his companion usually carries a *kongōsho,* or diamond pounder, an ancient Indian weapon that was so hard that it could crush even diamonds. There are three different types of this useful weapon, all replete with mystical significance, and the right-hand figure at Sugimoto-ji carries a pounder called a *dokko.* All of which can, I suppose, be safely consigned to the Department of Useless Information. But, on the other hand, it is difficult to reach any sort of real appreciation of Japanese religious art without some knowledge of the symbolism involved.

The temple is housed in an old thatched-roofed building, to the right of which are gathered in tumbled disarray scores of small tombstones commemorating (so it is said) warriors fallen in battle

◁ *One of the two guardian Niō-san statues at Sugimoto-ji.*

during Kamakura's stormy past. The inside of the temple contains a cheerful, cluttered profusion of ema votive tablets, colored paper decorations hanging from the ceiling, receipts of donations (one, I recently noticed, acknowledges with thanks a donation from the Mothers' Club of a local Christian kindergarten), pilgrim labels, and other dusty impedimenta. In fact, Sugimoto-ji is characterized by a happy, homey atmosphere that reminds me of Kiyomizu-dera, regarded as the "parish temple" of Kyoto. The origins of both foundations are lost in antiquity, and as a result both places transcend sectarian differences (Sugimoto-ji belongs to the Tendai sect) and attract pilgrims from the various schools of Japanese Buddhism.

The principal objects of veneration are three Kannon statues. Dozens of long white banners in the grounds proclaim "Shichimen Kannon" (Eleven-Face Kannon)—that is, Kannon depicted with ten smaller heads projecting out of the main head. This symbolism is again found in the Kannon statue at Hase (page 125) and represents the ten stages of enlightenment. In common estimation, however, the minor heads are looking in all directions so that the merciful and compassionate Kannon can hasten to the aid of people in distress. The three statues cannot be clearly seen from outside the sanctuary, but a polite word with the custodian seated behind the counter to the right is usually enough to allow the visitor to enter the sanctuary and make a closer inspection.

The oldest of the three statues supposedly dates from the Heian period (794–1192) and was carved by the monk Gyōki, who is said to have founded the temple. It is an extraordinarily fine piece of work, with a jewel set in the forehead and just a suggestion of a smile hovering on the lips. There are inevitably many stories attached to it. For example, when the temple was burned down in 1189, an attendant dashed into the roaring flames and rescued the statue without receiving the slightest burn himself thanks to the image's miraculous efficacy. It was also known as the Geba Kannon, or Get-Off-Your-Horse Kannon, for anybody daring to

Sugimoto-ji, with its banners reading "Jūichimen Sugi-moto Kannon" (The Eleven-Faced Kannon of Sugimoto).

ride past the temple gate without bothering to observe the courtesy of dismounting was invariably thrown off his horse. The other two statues of this triad date from a later period, although little or nothing is known for certain about their origin. But for centuries they have been the object of intense veneration; it is recorded that Yoritomo came here to worship in 1191 and his son Sanetomo in 1212.

Sugimoto-ji still attracts a host of pilgrims, some of whom are making the round of the thirty-three Kannon temples in the Kantō region, and the custodian obligingly stamps the seal-books of pilgrims and tourists alike as proof and souvenir of their visit. This ancient hillside temple is an interesting place because it enables you to catch an intimate glimpse of the workings of popular Buddhist religion and cult. This is a far cry from the passionless and disciplined Zen meditation as practiced in the monasteries of Kita-Kamakura, but it is an aspect of Japanese Buddhism that plays an important role in the religious life of the ordinary people.

Plans are afoot for completely rebuilding the temple, and one can only hope that Sugimoto-ji's cheerful, informal atmosphere will not suffer as a result. The thought of Sugimoto-ji being housed in a clinically clean and orderly modern building is too awful to contemplate. But the temple has been rebuilt many times during its long history, and prophecies of gloom have probably been expressed on each occasion. So I don't think there is much need to worry on that score—there will always be a homey Sugimoto-ji.

HŌKOKU-JI   This Rinzai Zen temple was founded by Ashikaga Ietoki in 1334, and its first priest was the monk Butsujō Zenji. This, at least, is one version, but Ietoki is thought to have died in 1317, seventeen years before the foundation. Uesugi Shigekane has been suggested instead as a candidate for the honor. Not that it matters a great deal to ordinary visitors, for they will find plenty to interest them when they call in at this temple.

As soon as you enter the grounds, you will notice the carefully raked patterns in the gravel to either side of the path, indicative of the temple's general air of prosperous activity. It wasn't always like this, for I can remember Hōkoku-ji when it was a nondescript, unvisited temple tucked away in the middle of nowhere as far as tourists were concerned. But the installation of a vigorous and imaginative resident priest some years ago has changed the picture completely, and Hōkoku-ji has become one of the best-known temples in Kamakura. This is true not only as regards tourism but also from the religious angle, for the temple organizes frequent sessions of zazen for laypeople, and these are well attended, especially by the younger generation.

The old thatched-roof belfry on the left side of the courtyard must date back for centuries, but the main temple building is relatively new. The *shoin* (literally, writing hall) on the right-hand side is obviously brand new, although constructed in traditional style. Exhibitions of calligraphy are held here, while in the basement floor is housed a large hall for zazen. A dry garden of gravel and rocks is located in the angle between the temple building and the writing hall, and visitors can enjoy a fine view of it from either of the buildings. And it is an attractive garden, far more pleasing than the gravel-and-rock garden in Kōmyō-ji.

But one of Hōkoku-ji's chief claims to fame is the bamboo garden at the rear, and the place has become known as the Bamboo Temple as a result. You have to pay to enter the enclosure, where you will see a dense miniature forest of these lovely trees, the ground covered with their fallen leaves. All this is new, having been produced within the past few years. Whether or not bamboo was growing there when I first visited the temple years ago I cannot now recall, but there was certainly nothing organized then on the present scale.

"Organized" is perhaps the relevant term here, for although I find the garden attractive (how could one fail to find it attractive with so much lovely bamboo in sight?), there is nevertheless a rather organized, self-conscious, artifical air about it. Although pleasing to the eye, the bamboo grove has a museumlike, do-not-touch atmosphere and lacks a certain natural spontaneity. The entrance fee into the garden, the booths serving green tea to visitors, the roped-off pathways, the electric lanterns set among the bamboo—all this I found a little offputting and overdone. It was with some relief that I viewed the old Ashikaga tombs set in the cliffside just before exiting. This type of thing seemed more in the traditional spirit of Kamakura.

Yet we can easily fall into a trap here, and it is unfair to expect and wish that everything in Kamakura should be slightly old and musty before it can be considered acceptable. This was obviously not true of Kamakura in the first century of its foundation as a city, for everything then was new and revolutionary compared to the staid conservatism of Kyoto. I have at times heard criticism of the present policy of this temple, and some people do not care for all the publicity it receives. There are, for instance, quite a few photos on prominent display in the temple building showing the visits of well-known personalities—a baseball star is seen chatting with the resident priest and then performing zazen under his direction. Recorded tapes of the priest's sermons and copies of his book on Zen are readily available.

But before one begins to criticize such activity, it would be as well to ask what is the fundamental purpose of the temple. To serve as a museum and repository of ancient religious art? To act as a nostalgic link with Kamakura's once-great past? Or rather to function as a religious center and try to give meaning to people's lives and help them with their basic problems? If this last is the true purpose of a Buddhist temple, then I would suggest that Hōkoku-ji, with its vigorous program of religious instruction and exercises for the laity, should rank rather high among the city's sixty-five temples. In this respect the next two or three temples further down the road offer a startling contrast.

JŌMYŌ-JI   This is the fifth of the Five Mountains temples, the five leading foundations of the Rinzai Zen sect. It was founded by Ashikaga Yoshikane in 1188, and so it is the only one of the five to have been inaugurated by a non-Hōjō patron. Its first abbot was the well-known monk Taikō Gyōyū. Gyōyū started his religious life professing mystical Shingon teaching, and this temple began its existence belonging to that school and was originally called Gokuraku-ji. When the patriarch Eisai visited Kamakura in 1199, Gyōyū turned to the Zen sect, but it was only sometime later that this temple changed both its denomination and name. Gyōyū was on close terms with Yoritomo, Masako, and Sanetomo. He managed also to be patronized by the Hōjō family and became the first priest of Tōshō-ji, where he died. It will be remembered that Tōshō-ji was the Hōjō family temple where Takatoki and his retainers committed mass suicide on the fall of Kamakura in 1333.

Jōmyō-ji had a succession of distinguished abbots and, as one of the Five Mountains temples, once possessed many buildings and enjoyed considerable prosperity. But fire and earthquake brought its splendor to nothing, and very little of its former eminence remains today. It still owns statues of Shaka Nyorai and Gyōyū, as well as various relics connected in some way with its patron family, the Ashikaga. And in recent years the spacious courtyard has been tidied up and put in order. But on the whole Jōmyō-ji presents a rather melancholy, deserted appearance, with no evident trace of its early affluence. Perhaps in this respect it is still serving a useful function, exemplifying the Buddhist teaching on the inevitable passing and decay of material things.

KŌSOKU-JI   This is a pleasant and interesting old temple located among the country houses of the Jūniso district. Just before you reach the temple, you will pass several ancient thatched houses that are still being used as residences. The temple is said to have been founded by the thirteenth-century monk Ippen, who began the Jishū Amida sect. Ippen began as a member of the Tendai sect, and it was only later, on account of a miraculous dream, that he turned to the cult of Amida. Kōsoku-ji is thought to have started as a Shingon temple, but to have changed its allegiance on account of Ippen. So it is far from clear in the records whether he took over an already founded temple or he himself inaugurated it.

The temple grounds are well worth a visit, especially for the quaint carvings on some of the tombstones in the cemetery in front of the building itself. There is also the Shioname Jizō statue to be seen in a wooden alcove by the pond. This battered stone figure received its peculiar name (literally, Salt-Tasting Jizō) because it used to stand nearby at the side of the road to Kanazawa, and salt merchants traveling along that route would leave small offerings of their wares so as to ensure good sales. An irate merchant, having failed to sell his goods, once knocked the statue over and stuffed its mouth with salt, and since then the old relic has been safely housed within the temple precincts. The tradition still continues to this day, and on a recent visit I noticed a fresh packet of salt ("Kitchen Salt. Net weight, 1 kg.") residing on its lap.

But there is an even more celebrated statue kept inside the temple building, and this will be shown on request. This is the Hōyake Amida, or Burned-Cheek Amida, and its story is related in an illustrated scroll preserved in the Kokuhōkan. It appears that there was once a pious lady named Machi no Tsubone, and she commissioned a sculptor (some say he was Unkei himself) to make a statue of Amida Buddha. This he did, and she duly enshrined the new image. During the lady's absence, however, Manzei, a priest who was a member of her household, was falsely accused of thieving and branded on his left cheek with a red-hot iron. In his agony he called upon Amida Buddha for help. As a result of his prayer all trace of the burn disappeared, and although his cruel tormenters renewed the torture, they were unable to do him any further injury.

Meanwhile the mistress of the house had a dream in which Amida appeared with a terrible burn on the left cheek. On her return to Kamakura, Machi no Tsubone found that her statue was branded on the cheek and blood was flowing from the wound—the loving Amida had accepted the torture of the falsely accused servant. Ever since then, despite the best efforts of repairers, this statue has had a burn scar on its left cheek. So we are told, although when I was kindly taken around the interior of the temple some years ago by the resident priest and shown the statue in question, the dim lighting inside its shrine made it difficult to verify the existence of the wound. But what does it matter? The purpose of the legend is to emphasize the lovingkindness of Amida Buddha and to instill devotion in the hearts of the faithful. This it does with undeniable success.

JŪNISO SHRINE   The Jūniso district marks the eastern limit of Kamakura City, and its name literally means Twelve Places. Why it should be called this is not known. Perhaps there used to be a dozen principal homesteads or farms in this area, or possibly a dozen small shrines after the fashion of the Kumano Twelve Shrines in western Japan (as we will see, there is a Kumano Shrine in this area). Whatever the reason for the name, if anybody corrects your pronunciation and tells you that the name should be read as Jūnisho, as in Gosho (Five Places) Shrine (see page 93) you can reply loftily that you are using the accepted local pronunciation— and if the local residents do not know how to pronounce the name, who does?

The shrine was founded in 1278 and was originally a fox shrine located in the confines of Kōsoku-ji until it was transferred to the present hillside site in 1838. Its enshrined patrons are the seven celestial and the five earthly deities (which numbers make a round dozen and may have something to do with the origin of its name), and its annual festival is observed on 9 September. Apart from that, what more can be said about Jūniso's local shrine? The two decrepit buildings look deserted and neglected and quite lifeless.

But then you notice the fresh offering of fruit in front of one of the locked sanctuaries. And you see the stream of people, clad in their best kimonos, trudging up the bumpy track at New Year's in order to present themselves before the parish shrine and ask for blessings and good fortune in the coming year. And as for the activity around the shrine every September on the occasion of its annual *matsuri,* or festival—well, that's another story altogether. The lesson to be learned, I would suggest, is that however dormant and dead Shinto may appear exteriorly, belief in the indigenous deities (if "deities" is the right word to use in this context) is still very much a living tradition in modern Japan.

ASAHINA PASS   If the Jūniso Shrine does not show much sign of life and is of scant interest to the casual visitor, it serves at least a useful purpose in that it marks the beginning of two trails. The path to the left leads into Ten'en Park, and so you can walk from this eastern part of Kamakura all the way to Kenchō-ji in Kita-Kamakura without crossing a single road and, as an additional bonus, enjoy some fine views of the surrounding countryside. And on the other side of the road there starts a path that will take you along my favorite Kamakura walk through the old Asahina Pass.

This was formerly one of the busiest entrances into the city, for it served as the vital route to the east, leading to present-day Chiba. Although Kamakura had its own port at Wakaejima in Zaimo-kuza, rough seas there were liable to prevent the smooth unlading of supplies, and so of necessity, goods were transported into the city through this pass from the port at nearby Rokuura. These goods included military supplies, salt from Chiba, and (so it is said) the materials for constructing the Great Buddha. The pass was deliberately kept narrow for defensive purposes, and it was inevitable that a new route would sooner or later have to be constructed over the hill to allow for the unimpeded flow of traffic. So the modern road leading out of the city climbs the steep hill, passes through Kamakura Reien (the new cemetery), and then down toward Kanazawa-Hakkei. Which means that the old route that skirted the hill and ran by the side of the incipient Nameri River is now deserted and overgrown. Which in turn means that it makes an ideal path for an afternoon stroll, although as parts of the route seldom get any sun, the going can be a little damp underfoot.

This is a very enjoyable walk for anybody who has some interest in Kamakura's past. It is said that the regent Hōjō Yasutoki ordered the construction of the pass in 1241, although a more fanciful account tells us that Asahina Saburō, a young man of truly remarkable strength, cut the pass singlehandedly in one night some years earlier. Whatever its origin, the pass is a fascinating place to walk through. Burial caves can be seen in the sides of the cliffs, and it is interesting to note the faults in the rock strata laid bare where the route has been driven through the hillside. There are also ruins of various unidentified buildings, mostly to the left of the path.

Halfway along the route you will come to a small spring on the left, and this is called Kajiwara Tachi Sensui, or the Kajiwara Sword-Washing Spring. Such an intriguing name must have a story behind it. It appears that the mansion of Taira Hirotsune stood close to here, and as he was Lord of Chiba (he is sometimes known as Chiba Hirotsune), this was a very convenient location as the Asahina Pass leads off in the general direction of Chiba. Hirotsune initially fought on the side of his Taira family, but later switched allegiance to Yoritomo and rendered him valuable service in military campaigns. But relations between the two men became strained, and Hirotsune was maliciously slandered by his enemies.

Enter the villain, one Kajiwara Kagetoki. He also had fought for the Taira before going over to Yoritomo's side. Pretending to believe that Hirotsune harbored treasonous plans against Yoritomo, Kagetoki attacked the Taira mansion in this place in 1183, slew Hirotsune, and then calmly washed the blood off his sword here in the spring. Belatedly learning of Hirotsune's innocence, Yoritomo later expressed his regret over the incident, but then, as far as the unfortunate victim was concerned, it was rather late in the day to repent. But Kagetoki eventually received his just deserts. It was he more than anybody else who poisoned Yoritomo's mind against Yoshitsune and thus set in motion the tragic campaign against the ruler's half brother. After the death of his protector, Yoritomo, in 1199, Kagetoki was driven out of Kamakura by people disgusted by his cunning schemes and was killed in Shizuoka in the following year.

A little further down the path, you come to a small waterfall on the right, and this is called Saburō's Waterfall; Hirotsune's mansion is thought to have been located just above the fall. It is only right and fitting that the herculean Asahina Saburō should be properly commemorated in the pass that he cut by himself in one night, and so this miniature waterfall is named for him.

The walk in the Asahina Pass is so quiet and peaceful now that it is hard to realize that this was once one of the most bustling and frequented routes into the city. Today all you can hear is the sound of birds singing and the distant boom of the bell of Kamakura Cemetery above to the left. Sometimes the muffled roar of the heavy traffic along the modern road can be heard, especially in the first part of the walk, but it all sounds very remote, and as you enter deeper and deeper into the pass the noise dwindles away and disappears completely.

There are a number of paths leading off to right and left, and I have yet to explore them all. But there is one you simply mustn't miss. It leads off to the right into a pine forest, and there is a notice there telling you that this is the approach to Kumano Shrine. The shrine is dedicated to Kumano Sanzan Daimyōjin, that is, the collective deities of the three great shrines at Kumano on the Kii Peninsula, and is said to have been founded by Yoritomo himself to defend his city from the malign northeastern quarter. It was subsequently rebuilt about the beginning of the eighteenth century by Katō Saemon.

And there you are. That's all I know and that's all you need to know. The approach leads quietly through a silent pine forest for some distance until you finally reach the shrine. Giant trees tower on either side and steps take you up to the old shrine itself. It looks very deserted and remote—surely nobody has been here for years and years. Another flight of rather steep steps cuts up the hillside from directly behind the shrine building; a less arduous flight of steps (often called Women's Steps in olden days, because the other, steeper steps were difficult to negotiate while wearing a kimono tightly wrapped around the legs; Chinese women were hobbled by footbinding, Japanese women by the kimono) can be found to the right.

Behind the pair of stone lion-dogs guarding against intruders, a surprise awaits you—a brand-new shrine building, looking fresh and splendid. Constructed in traditional style, perhaps it looks a little bit too new for its surroundings, but it will weather in the course of time and thus be assimilated into its natural setting. This is what Shinto is all about, I reflected as I returned along the path after a recent visit. In some ways it is nothing more than a manifestation of the Japanese people's love for and awe of the natural beauty of their country; and just as the dead winter fields give birth to a new fruitful spring, so Shinto follows suit and is ever renewing itself with fresh vigor.

The final stretch of the Asahina Pass squeezes through narrow defiles between overhanging cliffs and in places is no more than three or four meters in width. And then you emerge from the enchanted forest and find quaint old tombstones and markers on the left—and a less-than-lovely factory on your right. This is none other than Ōminato Kōgyō, and it produces refrigeration equipment, water pipes, and other necessities of the twentieth century. So with a jolt we are back now in the modern world—perhaps no bad thing, for it doesn't do to become oversentimental about the past.

Faithful reader, if you have come this far, I must tell you that we are now well outside the Kamakura city limits and into the outskirts of Kanazawa-Hakkei. You can either retrace your steps and walk all the way back through the Asahina Pass, or you can catch a bus. The buses going to the left will take you either to Ōfuna, or over the hill, past the cemetery, and back into Kamakura, while the ones going to the right will drop you off at Kanazawa-Hakkei Station.

Nichiren

Kamakura Station ___10 min.___ → Hongaku-ji ___10 min.___ →
本覚寺

Myōhon-ji ___10 min.___ → Jōei-ji ___5 min.___ →
妙本寺　　　　　　　　　　　常栄寺

Yagumo Shrine ___10 min.___ → An'yō-in ___10 min.___ →
八雲神社　　　　　　　　　　　安養院

Myōhō-ji ___5 min.___ → Ankokuron-ji ___15 min.___ → Chōshō-ji
妙法寺　　　　　　　　　安国論寺　　　　　　　　　　長勝寺

THROUGHOUT THE CITY's long history various outstanding religious figures have lived in or at least visited Kamakura. To name just a few examples: Musō Kokushi was the founder of Zuisen-ji; Bukkō Kokushi, the founder of Engaku-ji; and Daigaku Zenji, the founder of Kenchō-ji; not to mention Ninshō of Gokuraku-ji, and Ryōchū of Kōmyō-ji. Dōgen, the Sōtō Zen patriarch whose writings are very much under study at the present time, came to Kamakura in 1247 and during his six-month stay conferred with the fifth Hōjō regent, Tokiyori. Another distinguished visitor was the monk Eisai, who made two trips to China and introduced tea drinking into Japan on his return. He came to Kamakura in 1199 and, with the cooperation of Masako, founded Jufuku-ji in the following year; he later dedicated to Sanetomo a learned treatise listing and extolling the virtues of tea drinking.

All of these worthy men contributed to the religious life of Kamakura, yet none of them made a greater impact on the city than Nichiren. For one thing, Nichiren lived in Kamakura for some twenty years, preached openly in the streets, and mixed with the ordinary people. Whereas the Zen monks often served as trusted advisers to the Hōjō government, Nichiren clashed with the civil authorities on more than one occasion, was exiled twice, and narrowly escaped execution—all of which helped him to win a good deal of public sympathy. In addition, he was a strong personality and never hesitated to speak his mind bluntly.

Nichiren has earned for himself a unique position in the history of Japanese Buddhism in that he founded a completely Japanese sect. All the other sects—Tendai, Shingon, Jōdo, Zen—developed in China before being introduced into Japan. Their doctrines and practices were modified to suit the Japanese temperament, it is true, but nevertheless all of these schools originated abroad and were later imported into this country. The Nichiren sect alone is a purely Japanese product.

Nichiren was born in 1221 in what is now Chiba Prefecture. As a youth he became a monk and spent years diligently studying the doctrines of Zen, Tendai, and Shingon. Dissatisfied with their teachings, he began propagating his own message in 1253, emphasizing the overriding efficacy of the *Lotus Sutra* (Myōhōren-gekyō). Just as the members of the Jōdo sect put all their trust in the saving mercy of Amida Buddha and repeat the invocation *Namu Amida Butsu* (All Hail to Amida Buddha!), so in a somewhat similar fashion Nichiren's followers recite over and over again the sacred formula *Namu Myōhōrengekyō*. Nichiren's unorthodox views led to his expulsion from his native place, and so he came to Kamakura in 1253 and lived in a hermitage located to the right of Wakamiya Avenue as you walk toward Hachiman Shrine.

In 1260 Nichiren completed his famous treatise *Risshō Ankoku Ron* (On Maintaining Justice and a Peaceful Country) and presented a copy to Hōjō Tokiyori. This regent was a fervent member of the Zen sect and did not take kindly to Nichiren's outspoken criticism of the various schools of Buddhist teaching, and so the priest was exiled to Itō on the Izu Peninsula in the following year. Pardoned after three years, he made various journeys, returned to Kamakura, and aroused the enmity of other sects by his distinctly unecumenical attitude ("Jōdo is the path to hell, Zen the teaching of devils, Shingon will ruin the country"). The arrival of ambassadors from Kublai Khan demanding the submission of Japan made the Kamakura government understandably jittery, and in 1271 Nichiren's enemies contrived to have him condemned to death. The sentence was commuted at the last moment, and the patriarch was again packed off into exile, this time to the island of Sado.

The Mongol invasion attempt in 1274 seemed to bear out Nichiren's prophecies of doom, and he was once more pardoned. He spent most of his remaining years on Mount Minobu in Yamanashi Prefecture and died in 1282 at Ikegami, located in the south of present-day Tokyo.

Nichiren is certainly one of the most important figures in Japanese religious history, and his influence remains undiminished to this day. The widespread Sōka Gakkai sect, from which the Kōmeitō political party took its origin, bases its teachings on the doctrine of the Nichiren sect. Because of the founder's long and intimate association with Kamakura, it is hardly surprising that the Nichiren sect has a large number of temples in the city. Whereas most of the foundations to the left of Wakamiya Avenue (as you walk toward Hachiman Shrine) belong to the Rinzai Zen sect, those to the right of the avenue profess the teachings of the Nichiren sect. In fact, a monument on the road running parallel to Wakamiya Avenue marks the place where Nichiren used to preach to passersby in the street.

HONGAKU-JI   Hongaku-ji was founded by the monk Nisshutsu (most of Nichiren's early disciples took the first character of the patriarch's name, *nichi,* or its derivative, when they chose or had chosen for them their religious names) in 1436. Formerly a Tendai temple called Ebisudō stood on this site and the nearby bridge over the Namerigawa is still called Ebisudō Bridge. Nichiren is said to have stayed at this place before leaving Kamakura for Mount Minobu.

The temple bell has a rather nice legend attached to it. It is dated 1410 and originally belonged to the Hachiman Shrine in Kisarazu in Chiba—although what an obviously Buddhist bell was doing in that shrine in the first place is not made clear. At any rate, Nisshutsu took part in and won a religious debate there and claimed this bell as his prize. There remained the problem of transporting the trophy back to Kamakura, but fortunately among Nisshutsu's servants was a herculean fellow called Ishiwatari Shin'emon, who trudged all the way back from Chiba with the heavy bell on his back.

A further claim to fame for this temple is the tomb of Masamune, the master swordsmith, which is also located within the grounds. Presumably on account of this connection Hongaku-ji stages a swordmaking demonstration in its courtyard every year. I once came across this spectacle purely by accident and remained fascinated to see the traditionally robed smith hammering the red-hot metal into a sword. Behind him, standing on the alert, were representatives from Kamakura's fire department, they too clad in samurai-like costume, with their hoses ready in case stray sparks from the open furnace were blown on the nearby wooden buildings of the temple.

MYŌHON-JI   This is the largest Nichiren temple in the city and is said to have been founded in 1260. In keeping with its importance, a tall stone column marks the approach to the temple just across the Ebisudō Bridge. In addition to Myōhon-ji's name inscribed in large and bold characters, the sacred formula *Namu Myōhōren-gekyō* is also written in thin drooping letters. This type of inscription is called *hige-daimoku,* or mustache prayer, because the drooping strokes resemble a mustache, and it is peculiar to Nichiren temples. So even if you cannot read the actual characters, you can always tell a Nichiren temple when you see this odd style of writing displayed on a monument.

Myōhon-ji's setting at the end of the Hiki Valley is strikingly attractive, and, as it is within ten minutes' walk of the station, the place is readily accessible. Despite its closeness to the city center, however, the temple is usually very quiet and serene—except on one particular Sunday every autumn when the local kindergarten (located in the octagonal building just within the temple's first gate) holds its sports day in the grounds. But apart from this noisy but happy intrusion, the precincts preserve an atmosphere of tranquility and peace, with nothing to hear except the singing of the birds.

The valley was famous for its birds' songs way back in the Kamakura period. In 1277 Lady Abutsu traveled down to Kamakura in the hope of settling a property lawsuit and left on record that this valley was renowned for the song of the warbler. Poor Lady Abutsu! Being a Kyoto courtier she took the conventionally dim and disdainful view of Kamakura. She lodged near Gokuraku-ji and miserably complained of the dismal sound of the wind and the waves.

Myōhon-ji's pleasant setting gives little indication of the tragic events that took place here in the early thirteenth century. The valley takes its name from the native place of Yoritomo's nurse, who on her retirement came to live in this vicinity. She adopted her nephew Hiki Yoshikazu, and he rendered valuable service, both military and political, on behalf of the Minamoto family. Yoshikazu's daughter, Wakasa no Tsubone, bore the second shogun, Yoriie, a son named Ichiman. And that is how the tragedy began.

On Yoriie's falling sick in 1203, a dispute broke out over his succession, and Yoshikazu complained on behalf of his infant grandson, Ichiman. Masako informed her Hōjō kinsmen of Yoshikazu's dissatisfaction, and he was promptly assassinated. The Hiki family rose up in arms to defend themselves, but they were wiped out, together with a hundred members of their household, by Hōjō soldiers. Among those who perished when the Hiki mansion was burned down here in this valley was three-year-old Ichiman, and his tomb (called the Sleeve Mound, because nothing more than the sleeve of his small robe could be found after the fire) is to the left of the main gate of the temple. The other members of the Hiki family are commemorated by tombs just to the right of the main building. The temple, in fact, was founded by Hiki Daigaku Saburō, a son of Yoshikazu, so that prayers could be offered for the deceased members of his family.

There are other fine tombs in the precincts. Notice, for example, the massive five-tier example on the right-hand side of the main courtyard. Dated 1624 and bearing the name Kaga, this tomb must be one of the finest of its kind in the city. More recent graves are found in the cemetery on the left-hand side of the grounds; the graveyard is divided into two parts, one being near the main gate, the other to the left of the main building. At the far end of the former part is located the grave, suitably embellished with seashells, of Admiral Hikonojō Kamimura, a colorful and forceful personality who played a major role in the Japanese naval victories in the Russo-Japanese War, 1904–05.

The best overall view of the temple grounds may be gained by climbing up to the belfry near the main gate. With a bit of luck and skill it is possible to take some good photos here without including the concrete Reihōden building standing out like a sore thumb in the rustic surroundings. The main building, or *hondō*, is normally closed, and ordinary visitors cannot enter. It contains an ancient seated statue of Shaka Nyorai in its sanctuary. But even more valuable in the eyes of the faithful, and now preserved in the safety of the fireproof Reihōden, is a wooden statue of Nichiren; carved in the fourteenth century, it is considered to be one of the sect's three most sacred statues of the founder.

The Hiki Valley is one of the most pleasant spots in Kamakura. Small wonder, then, that the thirteenth-century poet-monk Senkaku chose this place to write his celebrated commentary on the *Man'yōshū,* the collection of poems compiled in the eighth century. Senkaku could hardly have picked a nicer place.

JŌEI-JI, YAGUMO SHRINE Within this district there are two other institutions—one temple and one shrine—that can be given but a passing mention. Jōei-ji was founded by Nisshō, one of the most important direct disciples of Nichiren. This small and unpretentious temple glories in the nickname Botamochi-dera, or Rice-Dumpling Temple, for it was here that a pious nun offered Nichiren a rice dumpling as he was being led off to execution in 1271.

The nearby Yagumo Shrine is one of four shrines in Kamakura all bearing the same name. It is the parish shrine of the Ōmachi district and celebrates its annual festival on 7 July. It is supposed to date from the eleventh century, but (as in the case of the Gosho Shrine in Zaimokuza; see page 93) it was amalgamated with other local shrines by the Meiji government in 1911. It now presents a very rundown appearance, and its only real point of interest is that the precincts mark the beginning of a hiking course across the hills (see page 145).

By the way, Yagumo means eight clouds, while Hachiman means eight banners, and it would be reasonable to expect that the word for "eight," written with the same character in both cases, would be pronounced in the same way in these two names. But no, that would be far too simple in Japanese. "Eight" in this shrine's name is pronounced as *ya* and in Hachiman's name as *hachi*. Don't ask me why—it just is.

AN'YŌ-IN   Although right in the middle of the Nichiren district, this temple belongs to the Jōdo sect. Originally called Chōraku-ji, it was founded by Masako in 1225, the year of her own death, in the Sasame Valley so that prayers could be offered for the repose of her late husband, Yoritomo. But the temple was destroyed when Kamakura was attacked in 1333, and so the foundation was later transferred to the present site, on which had formerly stood a temple called Zendō-ji, also burned down by military action. It was probably at this time that the temple was renamed An'yō-in, An'yō being Masako's posthumous Buddhist name.

In its pleasant interior the temple possesses statues of Amida Nyorai and the Thousand-Armed Kannon, and it is the third of the thirty-three temples in the Kantō region to be visited by pilgrims making the round of Kannon shrines. An old stone statue of Jizō, seated in a small wooden sanctuary to the left of the main gate, is called the Nichigen, or Time Limit, Jizō and is the object of veneration for women praying for an easy childbirth.

An'yō-in has a well-kept garden, an intriguing statue of Miga-wari (Substitute) Jizō featured lying underneath a counterpane, and a very fine tomb, dated 1308 and the oldest of its type in Kamakura. The tomb is reputed to be that of the monk Ryōben Songan, son of Hōjō Tomotoki and founder of Zendō-ji. I will have to use the word "reputed" once more when we turn to another nearby tomb that is said to be that of Masako herself, for Jufuku-ji, another temple founded by Masako, also claims her remains. It is not altogether impossible that her ashes were divided between the two temples to settle pious rivalry, but on the whole it is unlikely.

I recently had an amiable conversation with An'yō-in's custodian about this matter, and he admitted that nobody really knows where Masako is buried. For that matter, he added, there is also question about Yoritomo's final resting place, for the present tomb certainly does not date back to the time of his death. The doubt concerning his tomb is understandable because the rule of his Minamoto family was brief (for all intents and purposes, it ended with his death in 1199, because his two sons were not effective rulers), and it did not serve the purposes of the succeeding Hōjō family to perpetuate the memory of Yoritomo with too much zeal.

The case of Masako is somewhat different. She is one of the most famous women in the whole of Japanese history. Not only did she actively help Yoritomo to establish and maintain his hegemony, but also, after his death, she more than anyone else saw to it that the power vacuum was filled by her own Hōjō family. You would think that Masako, belonging to one important family by birth and to another by marriage, would deserve a fitting and indisputable resting place in Kamakura. But she labored under one big disadvantage—she was a woman. It is perhaps symptomatic of the subservient role allotted to women in the history of Japan (and other countries as well) that, despite her accomplishments, she is not suitably commemorated in Kamakura today. Come to think of it, of the hundreds of large and impressive tombs in the city, few belong to women. In fact, the only ones that come immediately to mind are those of the abbesses of Tōkei-ji and Eishō-ji.

MYŌHŌ-JI   Along with Kakuon-ji, this temple shares the distinction of being one of Kamakura's Buddhist institutions that most jealously guards its privacy. It is not always open to visitors, and there is a detailed list of rules and regulations—no small children, no food or drink, no shouting, no smoking, no picking flowers, no tripods—to be observed by all who manage to gain entrance. Strictly speaking, it is open only for *sankei,* or pilgrimage-like visits, rather than *kembutsu,* mere vulgar sightseeing, but the distinction between these two terms is not always easy to define.

Should there be nobody at the front gate, you enter the grounds, proceed to the temple office on the left, smite the hanging gong smartly, and await further developments. On my most recent visit I didn't have long to wait for these developments to occur. I was asked whether I had come for sankei and, if so, whether, as a non-Japanese, I could and had read the list of rules. I replied meekly in the affirmative, paid the ¥200 fee (Myōhō-ji is the only Nichiren temple in the city to charge admission), and then thankfully set off on my tour.

Nichiren lived in this place from his arrival in 1253, and a temple has stood here ever since his lifetime. Myōhō-ji was rebuilt in 1357 by the monk Nichiei, the bastard son of Prince Morinaga, who, it will be recalled, was imprisoned and then executed in 1335 at the cave behind Kamakura Shrine. Nichiei was the temple's fifth abbot, and it was he who changed its original name of Honkoku-ji to its present one.

The green-roofed temple building is rather lovely and was built thanks to the beneficence of the Hosokawa daimyo family at the beginning of the last century. Nowadays admission is not part of the ordinary tour, but fortunately I was shown around by the custodian years ago and still retain vivid memories of its profusely decorated walls, its sliding doors, and even its ceiling. The ceiling above the sanctuary is painted realistically with sea waves—a precaution against fire, the custodian remarked dryly. Elsewhere, colorful paintings depicting flowers, animals, and celestial beings brighten the interior. Even though you are not invited inside nowadays, there are postcards on sale showing some of these paintings.

In the center of the sanctuary there is placed a large gilt statue of Nichiren, while close by there is a smaller figure of the Buddha. (This is a characteristic set-up of the temples of this sect, and this personality cult keeps Nichiren very much in the minds of the faithful.) In a smaller room off to the right statues of Prince Morinaga and his posthumous son Nichiei, dressed in priest's robes, are enshrined in boxes.

The grounds of Myōhō-ji are beautiful—there is simply no other word to adequately describe them—and their beauty is enhanced not only by the natural surroundings but also by the temple's policy of regulating the admission of visitors. On an ordinary weekday you may well be the only person wandering quietly through the garden, up the steps, along the path, through the Niō gate, up more steps, and then up to the top of the hill at the rear. The Niō gate is an old thatched-roof structure, but the rude, red-painted statues within seem somehow to be vulgarly out of place in these peaceful surroundings. You then reach the foot of the most famous flight of steps in Kamakura.

These old steps are covered with moss and have earned for Myōhō-ji the nickname Koke-dera, or Moss Temple, in imitation of the more famous Koke-dera (Saihō-ji) in Kyoto. The moss-covered garden in Kyoto is in a class by itself, but Myōhō-ji's mossy steps have a charm of their own and present a quiet, somewhat nostalgic picture. There are about fifty of these steps, but climbing them would obviously damage the moss, so ascent is made by a parallel flight of more modern steps to the right. At the top of the steps stands an old wooden sanctuary called the Hokkedō, which contains a statue of Nichiren. The building is opened only twice a year, on 27 August and 12 September, that is, the days on which Nichiren was led to safety by a white monkey and was dramatically saved from execution at the last moment. The original Hokkedō was transferred to Kyoto as long ago as 1335, and the present building was constructed at the beginning of the last century by the Mito branch of the Tokugawa family. Myōhō-ji has certainly been fortunate in having such powerful and generous benefactors.

Yet another flight of old, broken-down steps leads to the top of the hill. The path to the right takes you to the memorial of Prince Morinaga, while that on the left ends in a small clearing in which stand the tombs of Nichiei and his mother, Minami no Kata. This lady was Morinaga's attendant during his imprisonment in Kamakura, and Nichiei was born as a result of their liaison. This scenic spot is supposed to have been one of Nichiren's favorite retreats while he was living in the locality.

But none of this historical information or written description can really do justice to Myōhō-ji or convey an adequate impression of its grounds. For a full appreciation you have to experience the place for yourself, not once but several times.

ANKOKURON-JI   This pleasant temple is built on the site of the place where Nichiren composed his controversial treatise *Risshō Ankoku Ron*—hence the temple's name. The cave in which he lived while writing the essay is to the right of the temple grounds. It was badly damaged in the Great Kantō Earthquake and now has a rather ugly plastic-roofed shelter erected in front of it. Just to the right, steep steps lead up the hill to the Fuji-Viewing Platform. I very much doubt whether the mountain is often visible from here except on cold winter mornings, but a somewhat uninspiring view of the city can be gained at all times—uninspiring, because all you can see is a vast area of drab roofs spread below you, and very little of Kamakura's natural beauty is in evidence.

The temple precincts are particularly well cared for, and both the flowers in spring and the *momiji,* or red maple leaves, in late autumn present an attractive sight. The cemetery lies to the right rear of the main temple building, and in the middle is found a small shrine marking the place where Nichirō, a direct disciple of Nichiren and one-time abbot of this temple, was cremated in 1320. A path leads through the cemetery into the hillside in the rear, past two enormous stone lanterns, one still standing but the other fallen, Ozymandias-like, to the ground, and finally to a large, rough-hewn cave called Chinmen no Iwaya. When an angry mob gathered to attack Nichiren's hermitage in 1260, a white monkey appeared and led him to safety from this cave over the hill and into the next valley. You can still follow this path over the top of the hill, but it is rough going and hardly recommended.

The temple building itself is a comparatively recent structure and is not open to the casual visitor. But Ankokuron-ji is set in pleasant surroundings and is well worth visiting.

Chōshō-ji "A pleasant, quietly run-down temple," I wrote in my notes when I first went to see this place years ago. At that time bulldozers were leveling off parts of the hill behind the temple, and the place was admittedly not looking at its best. So when I passed through Chōshō-ji's gates on a recent visit, I blinked in surprise. There stood a brand new temple building, with its decorative golden knob sparkling in the sunlight at the top of the fine roof and golden lanterns hanging down from the tips of the eaves.

Newly paved paths lead to the front of the building. Its exterior design is traditional, but the interior is somewhat out of the usual: the floor is covered with synthetic carpeting instead of tatami, and a pagodalike tabernacle on a low circular dais takes the place of the traditional sanctuary. In the courtyard four large celestial kings guard the new structure against wicked demons. With flowing robes and brandished weapons, each of these sentinels stands upon a discomforted devil. There is Zōchō in the front on the left (guarding the south), with Jikoku (east) by his side; behind them stand Kōmoku (west) and Tamon (north). These metal giants look very nice and suitably fierce, but I wonder whether they qualify as works of art. Perhaps it is because they still look so new and lack the patina of age—not a legitimate artistic criterion, heaven knows, but one has come to *expect* Kamakura's temples and statues to look old and slightly shabby.

So it comes as rather a relief to see that the Hundred Rounds marker is still there—the faithful can gain merit by making a hundred rounds of the temple. Also there are the Six Jizō, together with a rather charming Jizō with a baby in his arms, all of them muffled in caps, bibs, shawls, and scarves against the winter's chill. And the old Hokkedō hall, a venerable building in which services are still held, is there up the steps to the left.

A statue of Jizō and a child in the grounds of Chōshō-ji.

Chōshō-ji dates back to 1345, when another temple, Honkoku-ji, was transferred from this site to Kyoto and this Nichiren temple was built in its place. A man called Ishii Chōshō used to have his mansion here, and so the temple took its name from him. Perhaps the obvious present prosperity of Chōshō-ji has something to do with the recent construction of a new cemetery called Zaimoku Reien on the hill behind (*reien* can be translated as "spirit garden" and refers to modern non-denominational cemeteries; the traditional graveyard is called *bochi*). And although the modern reien is not nearly so attractive and interesting as the traditional bochi, it is worthwhile climbing up the steep steps to the top of the hill just to

see the view it commands. And what a fine view it is—the whole of
the city lies below, with the ocean to the left, the Hakone mountains in the middle background, and Mount Fuji there on the
horizon in the far distance.

Very much dominating the top of the hill is a new bronze statue
of Nichiren some four meters in height. To add to its dominance,
the figure stands on a pedestal eight meters in height. The artist has
captured some of Nichiren's characteristic attitude—strong, pug-
nacious, resolute, determined. Nothing dreamy or otherworldly
about this statue. "The statue looks down upon the city of
Kamakura," one Japanese-language guidebook informs us—
which is precisely what Nichiren *isn't* doing, for his back is
pointedly turned toward the city. I wonder why. It can't be just
accidental, as one does not commission such an enormous monument and then let it face haphazardly in any direction. Perhaps he
is facing the east (though I think that it is more like the northeast),
where the sun rises (the first character of his name means sun); or
perhaps he experienced such harsh treatment in Kamakura that he
prefers to turn his back on the city. I will have to ask and find out
one day.

Every year in the morning of 12 February a ceremony takes
place in the grounds of Chōshō-ji that inevitably attracts much
attention. In November of each year a group of Nichiren priests
begin a period of religious austerities on Mount Minobu, the
headquarters of the sect, lasting a hundred days. Observing a strict
fast and getting little sleep, they practice *mizu-gōri,* the penance of
pouring cold water over themselves, seven times a day. At the end
of their hundred days' ascetical exercises, they come to Kamakura
and go through the streets until they reach Chōshō-ji. They then
strip to their loincloths, and douse themselves with buckets of icy
water. Long-haired and bearded after their three-month retreat,
they perform this penance for world peace, and one could hardly
think of a more lofty and worthy purpose. The exercise takes place
in the temple courtyard, and you may go along to watch.

Zaimokuza District

Kamakura _10 min._ → Emmei-ji _20 min._ →
Station 延命寺

Myōchō-ji _10 min._ → Raigō-ji _5 min._ →
妙長寺 来迎寺

Gosho Shrine _10 min._ → Kuhon-ji _10 min._ →
五所神社 九品寺

Fudaraku-ji _10 min._ → Kōmyō-ji
補陀落寺 光明寺

THIS CHAPTER DEALS WITH the area known as Zaimokuza, that is, the district that extends to the left of Wakamiya Avenue as you walk from the station down toward the seashore. It is a large residential area, crisscrossed with narrow winding lanes and containing a number of small temples. Most of these foundations date back for hundreds of years and possess legends and ancient statues, yet with one or two exceptions they hold little of immediate interest for the casual visitor. Often enough they are locked up, and it is quite a job to hunt down the custodian and prevail upon him to open up the building. Even when the visitor is at last shown the dim interior, the effort seems to have been a little pointless, for there is not a great deal to see.

Not that this district is without historical interest. The very name

89

Zaimokuza means Lumber Merchants' Guild, and thus presumably at one time there was a good deal of lumber trade and carpentry carried on in this area. This trade probably went back to the Kamakura period, although the name itself appears to have come into use only during the Edo period. Before that, the district was known as Waka, or merely regarded as part of the Nagoe district to the immediate north.

It is more than likely that the lumber trade was connected with the fact that the port of Wakaejima was located at the eastern point of the present Zaimokuza beach. The port is considered to be Japan's first artificial harbor and was constructed in the summer of 1232. It was later repaired and renovated at various times, the most recent recorded date being as late as 1826. For a long time Wakaejima was a busy and flourishing port; sometimes at low tide a spit of land lies uncovered, and it is still possible to find shards of pottery (some of it imported from China) either in the shallow water or washed up on the beach. Somewhat less pleasant discoveries both here and elsewhere in Zaimokuza have been human bones and fragments of weapons, a grisly legacy of the bitter fighting that raged here when imperial troops stormed the city in 1333.

There is still a site that is called Midare-bashi, or Confusion Bridge, and this is where, after stubborn and heroic resistance lasting several days, the defenders began to waver and retire in confusion—hence the name. There is actually no bridge there now, and only a drainage ditch runs under the road at this point, but the name persists to the present day.

Nearby is situated a small shrine called Hachiman Kyōsha, or Old Hachiman Shrine, the former site of the city's biggest shrine. It is a matter of historical record that Minamoto Yoriyoshi built the structure near the beach in 1063, and it would appear that in those days the sea washed much further inland than at present. At the entrance to the narrow alley running to the small shrine there is a sturdy stone marker on which is recorded Moto Tsurugaoka

Hachimangū, or Original Tsurugaoka Hachiman Shrine, and there is even a bus stop of the same name in front of it. Considering that the shrine was transferred to its present site in 1180, eight hundred years ago, memories in Kamakura certainly go back a long, long time. By the way, you can't miss the stone marker as it is immediately next to a somewhat more recent foundation called the "Dog Beauty Salon."

Another place of historical interest is Geba-bashi, or Horse Dismounting Bridge, and the Geba crossroads, where the road from the Hase district crosses Wakamiya Avenue. In former times there used to be three bridges along Wakamiya Avenue: the Drum Bridge in front of Hachiman Shrine, another located close to the middle torii, and Geba-bashi. When an ordinary citizen rode on a horse or in a litter in olden days, he was obliged to dismount as a sign of respect when he passed in front of a palace or when he met a higher-ranking personage on the road. According to a stone monument, it was at these crossroads that Nichiren, while being led off to execution in 1271, turned toward Hachiman Shrine and in a loud voice called upon the gods to witness the truth of his religious message.

And it was here in this vicinity that a couple of disgruntled *rōnin,* or masterless samurai, hacked down and killed two Englishmen on 20 November 1864 in a display of xenophobic fervor. Major George Walter Baldwin and Lieutenant Robert Nicholas Bird, attached to the Twentieth Regiment guarding the Foreign Settlement at Yokohama, had ridden on horseback to visit Enoshima and had called in at the Great Buddha on their way back. Just as they reached this spot on Wakamiya Avenue, their assassins jumped out and slashed them down with their swords. If you ever visit the Foreign Cemetery in Yokohama, you can still see the gravestones of these two officers. As for their assailants, both were eventually arrested and executed by the Japanese authorities; one went fearlessly to his death, but his terrified companion had to be stupified with liquor to facilitate the proceedings. A rather remarkable, albeit gruesome, photograph still exists showing the head of one of the former samurai on public display in Yokohama—*pour encourager les autres,* I suppose.

EMMEI-JI   As mentioned, there are only one or two temples of real interest in Zaimokuza, but let me list just a few of the others for the sake of the record. Next to Geba-bashi is Emmei-ji, a temple of the Jōdo sect founded by the wife of Hōjō Tokiyori. The date of foundation is uncertain, but Tokiyori, the fifth Hōjō regent, died in 1263, and this gives us a rough idea of the period in which the temple was inaugurated. Emmei-ji has a highly decorated and orderly interior, and is worth a visit if only for its famous statue called Hadaka (Naked) Jizō. Whereby, of course, hangs a story.

Apparently a lady (according to one account, Tokiyori's wife herself) was once playing the dice game of *sugoroku* with a gentleman. Perhaps her partner wasn't really a gentleman, because he suggested that to enliven the proceedings the loser of the following game should undress and stand upon the sugoroku board. The silly woman agreed to play this type of strip sugoroku and (oh horror!) promptly lost the next round. In her distress she called upon Jizō to help her out of her embarrassing predicament, and Jizō appeared in female form and stood upon the board. To commemorate this remarkable occurrence, a statue was carved soon afterward and is preserved today on the left-hand side of the sanctuary. The image is vested in the red robes of a priest, but apparently does possess a woman's body. I was once kindly shown the statue by the resident priest, but had to be content with seeing it merely in its clothed form.

By the way, the statue is displayed on the 4th, 14th, and 24th days of each month. This system of dividing the month into ten-day periods is traditional in Japan and was observed until the more modern idea of the weekend was introduced. You can still find shops that are closed on the 3rd, 13th, and 23rd, or 5th, 15th, and 25th days of each month.

MYŌCHŌ-JI, RAIGŌ-JI Myōchō-ji was founded in 1299, and it is said that Nichiren stayed at this place prior to departing for exile in Itō in 1260. To commemorate this event, a tall monument stands in the front garden. It really is an ugly thing, disproportionately big for its cramped setting; perched in an ungainly way on four pods, it looks for all the world like a latter-day rocket just about to be blasted off into space.

Then there is the Shingon temple called Raigō-ji, founded by Yoritomo as a memorial to Miura Yoshiaki, who died in 1181 and whose tomb and statue are in the precincts. Kamakura is located at the top of the Miura Peninsula, and Yoshiaki's great-grandfather took the name of the region when he settled there in the eleventh century. The temple nowadays is rather dominated by the kindergarten in its grounds; two hens and an exotic bird gaze beadily out of their cages at the little children playing on the swings and slides. Yoshiaki's statue can be seen in a small sanctuary to the right, and immediately next to it are two large tombs. One of these is Yoshiaki's, while the other belongs to a seventeen-year-old boy-warrior, Tatara Shigeharu, killed in battle near Yuigahama beach.

GOSHO SHRINE Zaimoku's parish shrine, so to speak, is Gosho Shrine, a small, unpretentious building approached by a narrow path. Its name literally means Five Places Shrine. It was formerly named Mishima Shrine, but in 1908 it was merged with four other local shrines as part of the late-Meiji government's policy to amalgamate and thus more easily control Shinto shrines. Its annual festival is observed on 9 July, and the visitor can see its portable shrines, which are carried through the streets for the festival, in storage in an outbuilding.

It has some interesting old tombstones in the precincts, many of them decorated with the *san'en* motif, that is, the three monkeys who see, hear, and speak no evil. Some of these monuments are quite old (one is dated 1687), many are interesting, and most are Buddhist in inspiration. This is rather intriguing because, although for many centuries Buddhism and Shinto were united in the Ryōbu-Shinto school, the Meiji government insisted on strict separation in order to purify the indigenous religion. Whatever the reason, these stones appear to have been overlooked and still stand today in this old Shinto shrine.

KUHON-JI, FUDARAKU-JI   There is also Kuhon-ji, a Jōdo temple founded in 1336 under the patronage of Nitta Yoshisada to commemorate those who fell in the fierce fighting of 1333. It possesses three rather fine wooden statues of Amida and a stone one of Yakushi Nyōrai, the Healing Buddha. Yet another temple is Fudaraku-ji, founded in 1181. It consists of only one small building, recently renovated, but its claim to fame rests on the fact that Yoritomo founded the place for the monk Mongaku. This well-known priest was born as Endō Moritō in 1120, and how he received his monastic vocation is justly celebrated in folklore. He fell passionately in love with his cousin Kesa Gozen and planned to murder her husband, Minamoto Wataru. The faithful wife deliberately took her husband's place in the dark sleeping quarters and was slain by the importunate Endō. On discovering the identity of his victim, the murderer saw the error of his ways and became a monk. Later banished to Izu in 1179, he befriended his co-exile Yoritomo and was instrumental in obtaining imperial support for the renewal of the Minamoto military campaign against the Taira family. Yoritomo always treated Mongaku with much kindness, but after the shogun's death the monk continued the dangerous game of dabbling in politics and ended his life once more in exile, this time on Sado.

KŌMYŌ-JI   Kōmyō-ji is one of Kamakura's largest temples and the only one within the city that is next to the seashore. It is also one of the most important Jōdo temples in the Kantō region, although the Jōdo temple of Kōtoku-in, within whose grounds is seated the Great Buddha, attracts a hundred times more visitors. It

Kōmyō-ji, the only temple in Kamakura that overlooks the sea.

was founded by Hōjō Tsunetoki in 1243, and its first abbot was Ryōchū (his posthumous title was Kishū Zenji). This renowned monk first came to Kamakura in 1240 and was awarded the temple called Renge-ji (formerly known as Goshin-ji) in the Sasuke district of Kamakura, before the establishment was moved to its present site and renamed three years later. The foundation enjoyed the favor of successive Hōjō leaders, and Emperor Go-Tsuchimikado extended his patronage to it in 1495. At the beginning of the seventeenth century, Ieyasu, the first Tokugawa shogun, appointed it as the leading center of Jōdo instruction in the Kantō region.

Thanks to this long and varied patronage, Kōmyō-ji has flourished through the centuries and acquired considerable prestige. But as in the case of so many other Buddhist institutions in Kamakura, it presents a rather deserted appearance today, and by far the largest number of people passing through its gates are children taking a shortcut to the school located behind the temple. Yet appearances can be deceptive, and there is a good deal of unnoticed activity going on behind the scenes, as I had occasion to see when I once visited the temple's offices. The fact that extensive restoration work has recently been completed on some of the buildings within the grounds shows that Kōmyō-ji is still very much a thriving concern.

The main gate is an extremely fine structure; it dates from 1533 and was restored in 1847. It is well worth taking the time to look up at the intricate system of brackets supporting the heavy roof—so intricate in fact that one can only marvel at the consummate skill and technique of the Japanese carpenter. Unlike the ceremonial gates at the Zen temples in Kita-Kamakura, this one really *is* a gate and has three pairs of massive wooden doors that can bar the entrance to the temple.

Within the actual precincts a jumble of old tombstones fills the corner to the right. Here again it is worthwhile examining these relics closely. Most of them are quite anonymous and bear no inscription, but some of them carry interesting, and at times droll, depictions of standing, leaning, and sitting figures. Also to the right are memorials to those who died in the wars, one of them distinguished by an old military shell standing rather incongruously in front of it. There is also a memorial for deceased pets, thus showing that Buddhist compassion extends even to the animal world. The belfry must be one of the largest in the city, with carvings of fabulous beasts projecting from the beams at the four corners. Unfortunately the bell that it houses does not share the same impressive proportions; cast in 1647, it looks undersized and lonely in the lofty belfry.

Kōmyō-ji has two subtemples, one on either side of its broad courtyard. The one on the right is called Renjō-in and is thought to be an even older foundation than the main temple itself, for Ryōchū stayed here while the principal building was being constructed. The temple on the opposite side is Senju-in, or Thousand-

Arm Temple, so called because of its statue of the Thousand-Arm Kannon. Such statues do not in fact own a thousand arms; the figure normally possesses a main pair of arms, plus about a score of subsidiary ones emerging from the sides and holding various symbolic objects. This establishment served as a school of Buddhist theology and is still used as a seminar house for student acolytes.

The main temple building must be one of the largest in Kamakura and is decorated within with a profusion of gold-leaf ornamentation. The interior is quite gorgeous and extremely attractive, the only jarring note being (in my opinion) the carpet covering the tatami matting in front of the central altar, where a golden Amida Buddha sits in majestic state. From the left-hand side of the encircling veranda runs a raised, roofed gallery to the Founder's Hall and temple offices. These are well worth viewing, but unfortunately they (and also the main temple building) are not always open to the casual visitor. All is not lost, however, for Kōmyō-ji offers a luncheon service of *shōjin ryōri,* or vegetarian cooking. It is necessary to make a booking a week or so ahead of time, and you will not only experience traditional monastic fare but will also have the opportunity of entering a part of the temple not normally accessible to visitors.

The raised passageway to the Founder's Hall affords a pleasant view of the Founder's Garden, which was laid out in the early Edo period by Kobori Enshū, the celebrated master of the tea ceremony, flower arrangement, and landscape gardening. The garden is mostly taken up by a large pond; this tends to look a little drab and desolate in winter, but in June and July, when the mass of red lotuses are in full bloom, it presents a magnificent sight. And, as the hundred-and-one Japanese guidebooks never fail to point out, this forms a pleasing contrast to the white lotuses (white was the symbolic color of the Minamoto family) in the Gempei Pond at Hachiman Shrine.

On the right-hand side of the main temple building is yet another garden, constructed as recently as 1973. Although considerably smaller than the Founder's Garden, it has one considerable advantage in that it looks just the same in both winter and summer. This is because it is a dry garden, that is, it consists of an asymmetrical arrangement of gravel, gray rocks, and mossy mounds. Surrounded on three sides by a whitewashed wall, it is called Sanzon Goso no Niwa, or the Garden of the Three Divinities and Five Founders, for three of the boulders represent Amida and the two attendants, Kannon and Seishi, while five other rocks represent the five Amida patriarchs of China. You may sit on the balcony, look down on the small garden, and think deep thoughts.

This last remark is not meant to be cynical, but, try as I may, I have yet to feel any rapport with or attraction toward this work. It always seems to me contrived and overdone; its contents are too tensely crowded and reflect little feeling of peaceful relaxation. The modern tile work skirting the side nearest the balcony also is out of keeping and adds to the overall lack of harmony.

As befits such an important and old foundation, Kōmyō-ji possesses valuable treasures, religious and artistic, but these are not on display. Among its outstanding statues are those of Amida Buddha, the founder Ryōchū, and a seated Jizō (dated 1325). But even better known are its two illustrated scrolls, the *Taima Mandala* and the *Jōdo Goso,* both of which are on permanent loan to the Kokuhōkan in the grounds of Hachiman Shrine.

A path leads through the playground of the kindergarten on the right and up to the road above. If you continue walking up this road, through the tunnel, you will come to the rear of Kōmyō-ji and will enjoy a splendid view of the temple roofs, the city, the bay, Inamuragasaki, Enoshima, and (sometimes) Mount Fuji. This is one of the three best views that Kamakura has to offer, the other two being from Ten'en Park and Chōshō-ji. A large middle school stands on the cliff behind the temple, and a path on the left will take you to the secluded graveyard of Kōmyō-ji's abbots.

I like this place, despite the fact that I recently spent more than an hour there in the cold drizzle, my only companion being a silent

The tombs of the Naitō family, Kōmyō-ji.

artist seated under an umbrella, deftly sketching the lonely scene. The tombs stand around the whitewashed walls of the small L-shaped cemetery, Ryōchū's memorial appropriately enough being the largest and occupying the central position of honor. Apart from the *gorin*, or five-tier, tombs of the three most recent abbots, all the tombs are in the *muhōtō* form, that is, the largest part is oval in shape (hence this type is less formally called *rantō*, or egg tomb), and this kind is traditionally associated with monks. There is one more exception, for in the part on the left stands the tall tomb of the founder Hōjō Tsunetoki, the only layman to be buried in this small cemetery. And even that is not quite true, for this fourth Hōjō regent, tired of secular life and bitter political squabbles, resigned his office and took Buddhist orders, adopting the name Anraku, shortly before he died in 1246.

During its seven hundred years of existence, Kōmyō-ji has had a lot of abbots, but not all of them are interred in this quiet enclosure. The tomb of the 107th abbot is undated but appears to be the most recent; the 105th died in 1940, the 99th in 1931, the 83rd in 1821, the 78th in 1804, the 71st in 1772, the 68th in 1776. It is noticeable how many of these men died in the hot summer months when, I suppose, fever and other infectious diseases were rampant. There are certainly not nearly a hundred tombs in this cemetery, and I wonder where the missing abbots have been laid to rest. Not in the graveyard near the temple's front gate, for I made a special search there.

Back along the road, through the tunnel, is another cemetery; in fact, if you came up from the temple, through the kindergarten playground, you will have seen this one before reaching the abbots' graves. This is the burial place of the two branches of the Naitō daimyo family from Nobeoka in Hyūga and Unagaya in Iwashiro. The Naitō were long associated with Kōmyō-ji, and the temple has a wooden statue of Naitō Tadaoki, who died in 1674. It was during his lifetime that the tombs were transferred to this place from Reigan-ji, a temple in Edo, and here they remain, with additions, to this day, line upon line of them, seldom visited and long forgotten. Some of the tombs are rather splendid, with sacred Sanskrit letters incised on their surfaces. There were constructed over a long period of time—I have noticed various dates: 1693, 1703, 1712, 1766, 1806, 1813, and 1859. These tombs have attracted the attention of specialists, for they clearly show the development of tomb styles during the Edo period.

The Six Jizō standing on the right by the entrance are in a reasonably good state of preservation, but further inside the graveyard there are two other sets in very woebegone condition: heads have rolled, arms are missing, bodies inclined at crazy angles. The Naitō tombs themselves are fairly well kept up and preserved.

Although flanked by houses on either side, this cemetery is one of the loneliest spots in the whole of Kamakura. I visited Kōmyō-ji regularly for years without realizing its existence, and came across the place one day by accident. I have yet to see anybody else inside the graveyard, although presumably people do visit it out of curiosity or piety. Despite its pleasant setting, within full view of the ocean, the Naitō cemetery invariably gives me a feeling of chill and unease. *Kimochi ga warui,* as Japanese people would say. Why I should feel like this is difficult to express. Perhaps it is because of the way these once-proud tombs are so crowded together, regimented side-by-side in unimaginative rows, museumlike, deserted, unvisited, forgotten, unloved.

But the very opposite feeling is much in evidence during Kōmyō-ji's annual festival, and so let us end this chapter on a happier note. The festival is called *Jūya,* or Ten Nights. The original idea was to hold special religious devotions over 6–15 October, but in these degenerate days this period has been reduced to 12–15 October. During these four days the usually quiet neighborhood suddenly teems with activity, invaded by crowds who come to visit the temple and walk around the hundreds of stalls set up in and around the grounds. The booths sell pretty well everything imaginable (and, for the non-Japanese, a good many things unimaginable as well), but the speciality is potted plants.

The festival is, after all, religious in origin and inspiration, and much activity continues both day and night within the temple itself. The sacred invocation *Namu Amida Butsu* is chanted hour after hour, sermons are preached, processions are organized, bells are rung, incense smoke billows sweetly within the hall. There is a constant coming and going of people who pay a brief visit before the sanctuary and then go off to enjoy the more mundane pleasures of the fair outside. But in addition to these transients, there remains throughout the night a stable group (myself included on one occasion) sitting, watching, listening, and dozing. It is a memorable experience and much to be recommended.

Hills to the West

Kamakura ____15 min.____→ Jufuku-ji ____15 min.____→
Station   寿福寺

Kuzuharagaoka Shrine ____10 min.____→ Zen'i-arai Benten ____15 min.____→
葛原岡神社   銭洗弁天

Sasuke no Inari Shrine ____35 min.____→ Kaizō-ji ____15 min.____→
佐助稲荷神社   海蔵寺

Eishō-ji ____15 min.____→ Jōkōmyō-ji
英勝寺   浄光明寺

NOW WE TURN TO the western part of central Kamakura, that is, the district that you enter upon leaving the station from the rear exit. Succeeding chapters will cover areas that lie further afield to the west—the Great Buddha, for example, and Enoshima. The district described in this chapter contains a mixed bag of temples and shrines. There is the Five Mountains temple of Jufuku-ji (the oldest Zen foundation in the city) and the popular folk-religion complex of shrines called Zen'i-arai Benten; there is Kamakura's only surviving Buddhist convent still inhabited by nuns and the fox shrine associated with Ugajin, patron deity of rice and fertility. For good measure there are also a couple of hilltop parks that you probably would not find without a guide. But all these disparate temples, shrines, and parks have one thing in common—they can all be easily reached on foot from the station.

JUFUKU-JI   Jufuku-ji, or to give it its full formal title, Kikokuzan Jufuku Kongō Zen-ji (all the temples have these long titles, but fortunately they are abridged in everyday use), is the third of the Five Mountains temples in Kamakura, although in fact it is the oldest Zen foundation in the city. Only recently I read that Jufuku-ji is actually the oldest Zen temple in the whole of Japan—a claim that surprised me, but on investigation it would seem to have some validity. For the temple was constructed here in 1200, and the patriarch Eisai was its first priest. Eisai did not immediately start teaching orthodox Zen after returning from China, and it appears that Jufuku-ji began its existence as an eclectic Tendai/Shingon establishment, and only later, in the time of its sixth and eighth abbots, Daikyū Shōnen and Nanzan Shiun, did it propagate pure Zen teaching.

Eisai went on to found Kennin-ji in Kyoto in 1202, which was a Zen temple from the very beginning. So perhaps we can say that Jufuku-ji is the oldest Zen temple, but that Kennin-ji, *qua* Zen temple, has a longer history.

At any rate, Minamoto Yoshitomo, Yoritomo's father, built a mansion on this site about 1144, and when his son entered the city in 1180 he planned to have his headquarters in the same place. A memorial hall for his late father was erected before it was realized that the site was far too small and cramped for the purpose, and alternative plans were made to have the general's palace built in another part of the city. But in 1200, a year after Yoritomo's death, his widow Masako inaugurated Jufuku-ji here so that services could be held for her late husband. So this place is sacred to the memory of both Yoshitomo and Yoritomo.

Thanks to Masako's patronage and Eisai's fame, Jufuku-ji flourished in its early years. A frequent visitor was Sanetomo, who came to consult with Eisai on religious matters. In order to popularize the drinking of tea, the monk wrote a famous treatise, *Kissa Yojōki,* dedicating it to Sanetomo; tradition says that Eisai composed the essay here at Jufuku-ji, and the temple possesses an early copy of the work. In the essay Eisai lists the many benefits of tea drinking and stresses its usefulness in helping Zen monks from becoming drowsy during their long sessions of zazen. But, inevitably, later commentators have seized upon one particular benefit mentioned by Eisai—that tea is a great cure for a hangover on the morning after the night before.

Eisai's successor as head priest was Taikō Gyōyū, who, it will be remembered, was the first priest of Jōmyō-ji and so was probably the only man to be abbot of two of Kamakura's Five Mountains temples. But Jufuku-ji suffered more than its fair share of fires, the temple being badly damaged in 1247, 1323, and 1467. As a result, both its importance and the extent of its property decreased radically, and today there is not a great deal for the visitor to see.

In front of the main gate there still stands an old *gebatō,* a stone marker telling riders to dismount from their horses before proceeding any further. The tree-lined paved path running up to the main temple building has a quiet charm and is often featured in photographs of Kamakura. In fact there is little else to photograph—just the main building, the belfry, and the temple offices. The sanctuary dates from the 1750s and possesses, but does not display, statues of Shaka Nyorai, the founder Eisai, and two Niō kings; its fine statue of Jizō is preserved in the Kokuhōkan at Hachiman Shrine.

The most interesting place in Jufuku-ji today is undoubtedly the old cemetery, located to the left behind the temple buildings. The main entrance has recently been closed owing to the danger of falling rocks, but alternative entrances are clearly signposted. Near the original entrance of this sprawling graveyard is a cave containing the tomb of Masako, the foundress; another cavern nearby houses the tomb of her assassinated son, Sanetomo. Well, so it is said, but Masako also has a tomb in An'yō-in (page 81), and nobody can be quite sure where she is buried. But as she founded and patronized the important Jufuku-ji, this temple would seem to be the most logical place for her to be buried.

Nearby is the tomb of the Mutsu family, where the remains of Munemitsu Mutsu, his son Hirokichi, and daughter-in-law Iso are enshrined. Munemitsu Mutsu was foreign minister in the 1890s, while Iso was the Englishwoman who loved and knew Kamakura so well, and who wrote *Kamakura, Fact and Legend.* She died in May 1930 and now rests in, to use her own words, this "tranquil and beautiful spot." Another interesting person buried here has a tombstone on which are inscribed the characters "Great Buddha." So his name must have been pronounced "Daibutsu," you say. Not at all, for he was the author Jirō Ōsaragi, most noted for his novel *Kikyō* (Homecoming), who died 1972. He was born in Yokohama in 1897 and started off life as Kiyohiko Nojiri, only later adopting the pen name Ōsaragi. But why should this name be written with the same characters as are used for "Daibutsu"? It's rather as if a man called Smith decides to adopt the pen name Jones, but insists upon spelling it as B-r-o-w-n. Impossible in English, but nothing is impossible in Japanese.

Apparently there was once a samurai called Ōsaragi Sadanao, who was killed during the 1333 fighting in Kamakura. He had lived behind the Great Buddha and had grown so fond of the monument that he used the characters *dai* and *butsu* to write his own name. So when Kiyohiko Nojiri went to live behind the Daibutsu in 1922 and when he chose a pen name, he had a clear precedent for adopting the name Ōsaragi and writing it as "Daibutsu."

Up on a small plateau, in the southwest corner of the cemetery, stands the tall memorial stone of the de Becker family. J. E. de Becker, born in England in 1863, arrived in Yokohama in 1887, and his family for long lived in Kamakura. Back in 1899, he published anonymously *The Nightless City,* a book about the Yoshiwara district (the former pleasure quarters in Edo) that raised a few eyebrows among the foreign community.

The path above this tomb leads into Genji Park and on to Zen'i-arai Benten, and so provides a convenient shortcut. On the right of this path you will see the cemetery of the convent Eishō-ji. This Genji Park, by the way, is a comparatively new creation, and I can still remember the area as a wild hilltop. All credit to the local authorities for laying out a pleasant recreational spot with lawns and cherry trees. It's a good place to stroll, with fine views, plenty of fresh air, and lots of space for children to run around and enjoy themselves.

KUZUHARAGAOKA SHRINE Contiguous to Genji Park is yet another open space, this one called Kuzuharagaoka Park (the name is easier to read when divided up as Kuzu-hara-ga-oka, meaning, literally, the Hill of the Kuzu [Arrowroot] Plain). This is a very old part of the city, for not only are there ancient burial caves near here, but prehistoric remains have also been found in the area. The shrine itself is of no particular interest. It was erected in 1887, and, as in the case of Kamakura Shrine, it honors an imperial loyalist who was executed here in the 1330s. The man in question was Hino Toshimoto, and his tomb, or memorial, is located near to the shrine.

Toshimoto was an official belonging to the court of the ambitious Emperor Go-Daigo, and his violent death was the result of poor timing. Wishing to take advantage of the increasing weakness of the Hōjō regime, the emperor commissioned Toshimoto to drum up military support for the imperial cause as remote preparation for a showdown with the Kamakura government. The loyal Toshimoto followed instructions, but the Hōjō authorities got wind of his activities and had him brought to Kamakura under arrest. Here he was duly executed in 1332 by order of the last Hōjō regent, Takatoki, who himself was to come to a violent end only a year later when imperial troops stormed Kamakura. The tragedy of Toshimoto's sad end was that the time was not quite ripe for imperial restoration. True, within a matter of months the Hōjō government would collapse and the emperor's cause would triumph. But by then it was too late for Toshimoto, who had already been sacrificed for the sake of the throne.

The *Taiheiki* provides us with a long and moving account of Toshimoto's last days. Very probably this lyrical version is not historically accurate in all respects, but it at least conveys to us, six centuries later, some feeling of the tragic fate that befell the loyal courtier. It is only too easy for us today to view a tomb dating from those far-distant times and have no notion of the drama and personal suffering involved.

One of the most celebrated passages in the *Taiheiki* describes at length the prisoner's journey from Kyoto to Kamakura as he passed through places of historical and literary interest. Even when he reached his final destination, Toshimoto's captors continued to show compassion toward the condemned man. He had vowed some time previously to recite aloud the *Lotus Sutra* six hundred times as an act of piety, and his sentence was postponed for some days to enable him to fulfill his promise. When the time finally came for his execution, he was carried in a closed litter up the Kewaizaka Pass into the place called Kuzuharagaoka, and here he was confined in a site screened off by curtains from public view.

His former attendant, a man called Sukemitsu, had hurried from Kyoto to see his lord before the sentence was carried out, and he was allowed to enter the screened-off area and deliver to Toshimoto a message from his wife. The condemned man called for writing materials and entrusted his reply, together with a lock of his hair, to Sukemitsu. He calmly wrote his farewell poem, referring to the Buddhist teaching of the evanescence of all worldly things. He then leaned forward, and his head was struck off.

Sukemitsu returned to Kyoto and delivered his master's last message. The grief-stricken widow became a nun, while the faithful attendant retired to Mount Kōya to lead the life of a monk. When you learn of the story of Toshimoto, somehow or other a bit of the attraction of Kuzuharagaoka Park momentarily fades and the place becomes rather bleak.

When you come to leave this place, you have a remarkable number of paths to choose from. You can take the path leading to the Great Buddha or the one going down to Kita-Kamakura. Or you can descend the Kewaizaka Pass and come out near Kaizō-ji. Or else you can walk through Genji Park and then go down through either Eishō-ji's cemetery or Jufuku-ji's. But why not take the slope down to Zen'i-arai Benten, for this is the place next to be described?

ZEN'I-ARAI BENTEN This fascinating shrine complex, whose name can be translated as Money-Washing Benten, is a little bit off the beaten track, and foreign visitors may have trouble finding the place on their first visit. It is doubtful whether Japanese visitors experience the same difficulty, for the route to the shrine is generously signposted (in Japanese) all the way from the rear exit of Kamakura Station. People are said to come all the way from Osaka just to pay their respects at this shrine, and on days of the Snake (according to the old zodiacal calendar) all you need do is follow the crowd and you are sure to land up at the right place.

The main entrance is through a tunnel cut into the hillside and then through another tunnel of wooden torii archways. There is also a rear entrance, again torii-tunneled, that I believe dates back only to 1958. There is a winding path from above as well, but this seems to be seldom used. Inside the hill-surrounded enclosure you will find a happy jumble of shrines, sanctuaries, altars, caves, ponds, palmists, and fortunetellers. It is quite impossible to describe the spot adequately—you have to go there yourself to experience the atmosphere pervading this folk-religion shrine.

They say that it all dates back to Yoritomo. In 1185 he had a dream on a day of the Snake in the month of the Snake (and I have

Washing money at Zen'i-arai Benten.

checked that 1185 was also a year of the Snake), and he was told that his future regime would greatly flourish if a shrine were constructed at a certain spring in Kamakura. No sooner dreamed than done. Yoritomo sought out the place and arranged for Benten to be enshrined there. At some time or other it was discovered that this was no ordinary spring, for money washed therein would soon double in value. Understandably enough, this remarkable property of the water exerted, and still exerts to this day, an irresistible attraction to people of all classes, ages, and occupations. Hence the visitors from Osaka.

The process of washing money has now been reduced to a fine art. You enter the main cave, take one of the small wicker baskets provided for the purpose, put the coins inside, and swill them around in the water. Bills can also be washed in this way and later dried in the warm incense smoke outside. I once inquired whether the same gratifying results could be obtained with foreign money and was assured that they would. However, my informant continued, you mustn't hoard the washed money and treat it as something special, but you must spend it just like any other money. I was about to ask whether it would be in order to rinse traveler's checks and credit cards as well, but fearing that this might be considered facetious, I resisted the temptation and said no more.

The complex of shrines is associated with Benten (also called Benzaiten), the only female among the *shichi fukujin,* the seven deities of good fortune. She is the patron of music, eloquence, beauty, and the arts, and is often depicted playing a lute (the naked Benten in the Kokuhōkan is one such example). For some reason, possibly because the music of the lute is said to sound sweeter over water, she is invariably associated with water, and her shrines are found on islands (the island in Shinobazu Pond in Tokyo's Ueno Park, for example) or in grottos by the side of rivers, lakes, or the sea (one of the best-known Benten shrines is in the large cave on Enoshima).

Exactly how Benten came to be associated with snakes is not known for certain, but it probably harkens back to the Indian origin of this deity. Sometimes snakes can be seen emerging from the intricate crown or hair decoration she wears on her head. Because of this connection you will see offerings of eggs and sakè here, for these are the snake's favorite victuals. Moreover, there is a remarkable statue of Ugajin, deity of grain and fertility, in the cave of this shrine, although unfortunately it is usually hidden behind the mountain of miniature torii left behind as ex-voto offerings. As a result, this statue can be viewed only when the ex-votos are periodically removed to make room for further offerings, and despite my repeated visits I have managed to see it only once. There was Ugajin, with a scowling human face but with the body of a cobra, emerging out of a vertical tree trunk. Purifying fresh salt was scattered around it.

It was a remarkable experience for me, as two elderly kimono-clad ladies were standing before the statue, both reciting fervently *Namu Myōhōrengekyō* (yes, truly), with one hitting the other on her back in time with the chanting. Behind them was a very

The snake statue of Ugajin at Zen'i-arai Benten.

elegantly dressed girl, a copy of *Vogue* tucked under her arm, equally immersed in her devotions. I couldn't help marveling at the varieties of religious experience that Kamakura had to offer—from the rarified atmosphere of the zazen halls of Kita-Kamakura to popular folk cult centering around Ugajin depicted as a cobra. The sight of the snake statue also brought home to me the fact that Buddhism is fundamentally an offshoot of Hinduism and that the Indian element can be found not far below the surface of popular cult.

Despite its name, I believe that the shrine complex is actually dedicated to Ugajin, with Benten playing only a subsidiary role. But such theological niceties don't seem to worry the thousands of people who flock to Zen'i-arai Benten, and quite rightly so.

Certainly the snake is much in evidence here, and I once noticed an old lady who had set up a stall outside the entrance tunnel and was selling dead snakes. What fascinated me was the mincing machine clamped to the counter—do people buy minced snake meat? I waited a good fifteen minutes to see her make a sale and use the mincing machine. But alas for her and for me, no customers came, and I had to leave without my curiosity satisfied.

A visit to Zen'i-arai Benten is much to be recommended. Just wander around and enjoy yourself—go into the cave and wash your money, visit the different shrines, have your fortune told if you wish, admire the plump carp in the pond, and treat yourself to a simple meal in one of the restaurants within the enclosure. But one piece of advice—when the time comes to pay the restaurant bill, *don't* (as some of my student visitors have done) offer mine host half the money due and wittily suggest that he wash it in the nearby spring and in this way receive the full amount. If he's heard this brilliant suggestion once, he's heard it a thousand times.

SASUKE NO INARI SHRINE   At the bottom of the steep slope leading up to Zen'i-Arai Benten you will find a narrow lane winding off to a rather similar shrine, Sasuke no Inari Shrine. The way to this shrine seemed so modest and unprepossessing that it was only recently that I paid my first visit to the shrine, and I still have fond pleasant memories of that day. What I had imagined would be just a short approach to a small shrine turned out to be a long walk through a tunnel of scores of torii—old ones, new ones, wooden ones, stone ones, red ones, unpainted ones—perched on the meandering hillside path and eventually leading to the fox shrine. The buildings themselves are nothing special, although the surrounding scenery is attractive. And to be seen on all sides are stone statues and china figures of foxes. Often enough in popular belief the fox itself is considered to be the deity in fox shrines, but in fact he is only the swift messenger of the patron deity of rice, who may be the same Ugajin whom we saw (or probably didn't see) depicted as a snake in nearby Zen'i-arai Benten. But the literature and theories concerning the fox cult are so extensive and numerous that it is better not to enter into this subject here.

This shrine is inevitably connected with Yoritomo as well. After all, he is Kamakura's favorite son, and so it does no harm to establish some sort of relationship, however tenuous it may be, with the great man. Yoritomo had another dream, this time while he was still languishing in exile in Izu, and he was told that the god of this ancient shrine would protect his interests when he established his headquarters in Kamakura. So when the general set up his regime here in Kamakura, he had his lieutenant Hatakeyama Shigetada reestablish this hillside shrine, and here it has been in this quiet secluded valley ever since.

If you follow the path leading up the hill behind the shrine building, you will eventually reach the hiking course to the Great Buddha. There you turn left if you wish to go to that monument, and right if you want to go to Kuzuharagaoka Park, Zen'i-arai Benten, or Kita-Kamakura.

KAIZŌ-JI   This temple, set at the end of the Ōgigayatsu Valley, is a pleasant place to call in on an afternoon walk. Its secluded location and quiet surroundings imbue it with a peaceful atmosphere, and even if there is not a great deal to be seen, Kaizō-ji is worth a visit.

The temple seems to have begun its existence as a Shingon foundation, but was later reestablished by Uesugi Ujisada in 1394 and became a Zen temple under the aegis of Kenchō-ji. Its first priest was a monk named Gennō, who is supposed to have invented the *gennō*-type hammer that is still in use today. The grounds are well kept and attractive. In front of the main gate is still a gebatō marker warning riders to dismount from their horses, while to the right is the Sokonuke Well. *Sokonuke* can be translated as "bottomless," although the word does not refer to the well as such, but rather to a poem composed by a nun who attained enlightenment as she drew water from the spring. The verse mentions a symbolic bottomless bucket with which to draw water, and it was from this reference that the well takes its name.

The main building in the center of the courtyard here was reconstructed in 1925 after the Great Kantō Earthquake, and its interior walls are decorated with paintings of dragons that had been executed by the artist Kanō Tanshin, who died in 1825. With its sanctuary almost tucked away in a sort of alcove that can be sealed off with sliding doors, this room looks like the chamber of a mansion rather than a temple interior. On the left of the courtyard you see a small, rustic building, transferred from Jōchi-ji in 1776. In the center of this dim, clay-floored hall is enshrined a golden statue of the seated Yakushi Nyorai, while to the left is another example of the Kamakura-period realistic depiction of a seated monk, Gennō, the first priest. Kaizō-ji, in fact, possesses quite a few interesting statues—Benten, Jizō, Kannon, Shaka Nyorai, and Garanjin (temple guardian)—but these are not always on public display.

The priest's quarters are on the right-hand side of the courtyard and occupy an old thatched-roof building. Here you have to apply if you wish to inspect one of the most famous caves in Kamakura. You pay the small fee and are lent a key, and then you follow the signposted route around the front, unlock the door in the cliffside, and enter the cave of the sixteen wells. It is advisable not to enter before your eyes have grown accustomed to the gloom inside, otherwise you run the risk of putting your foot straight into one of the pools of water, as I did on a recent visit.

The Jūroku Ido Yagura, the Cave of the Sixteen Wells, is a square stone chamber, and into its floor are set with almost geometric precision sixteen wells in four lines of four. I am not sure whether "well" is quite the right word to use in this context, for the springs seem more like shallow water-filled depressions in the rock floor. Whether or not the water seeps up into all of them is also doubtful, because it looks as if the pools are connected by a trickle, with the water passing from one to the next. Over the years the faithful have cast money into these pools, and many of the coins have congealed and are stuck to the bottom.

The whole area is full of burial caves, by the way; there is even one containing a snake statue of Ugajin. If you follow the lane that passes in front of the Sokonuke Well, you will notice a lot of caves, both natural and artificial, in the sides of the cliffs, and you even have to pass through a cavelike tunnel on the way.

That is all there is to be seen at Kaizō-ji. Nothing very momentous, admittedly, but it is a peaceful and charming place.

EISHŌ-JI, JŌKŌMYŌ-JI   Among the temples in this area that have not been described in this account are two that should be at least listed for the sake of the record. As this chapter has gone on long enough and as the casual visitor will not be able to see a great deal in either establishment, let me just mention these two places.

Eishō-ji is said to be Kamakura's only Buddhist convent in which nuns are still residing. It is located on the site of a mansion belonging to Ōta Sukenaga, who in 1456 built Edo Castle and thus set in motion the process that turned a small and insignificant fishing village into present-day Tokyo. A year later, he became a monk, adopting the name Dōkan, and so he is usually referred to as Ōta Dōkan in books. His tomb, by the way, is in the cemetery of Jufuku-ji, just next door.

One of his descendants, the daughter of Ōta Yasusuke, was a court lady named Katchi no Tsubone, and she bore the shogun Tokugawa Ieyasu his ninth son, Yorifusa, the founder of the Mito branch of the Tokugawa family. On the death of her patron she became a nun, taking the religious name Eishōin (the *shō* of this name and *katchi* of her former name are both written with the same character). This Jōdo nunnery was founded in 1636, and her granddaughter from Mito became the first abbess. Eishōin herself died six years later and was buried here.

The sanctuary dates from the temple's foundation, but of greater interest is the *shidō,* a sort of annex in front of the foundress's tomb. This one-room structure was built in 1643 and enables visitors to pay their respects to the tomb in comfort. Vividly painted in black and gold, its decoration probably owes something to the style of Ieyasu's mausoleum in Nikkō. The grounds of the temple are noted for their variety of colorful flowers, especially plum blossom in early spring. Years ago I was once given a two-hour tour of the establishment by a member of the small religious community residing here, and I fortunately took notes at the time. I rather think that such a tour is no longer possible.

But you can still visit the convent's cemetery on the hillside behind. It is laid out in two parts, the upper one of which lies alongside the path running from Jufuku-ji's cemetery to Genji Park. This upper section contains the graves of local residents and has an attractive statue of Jizō gazing down benignly on the scene. Long, winding flights of steps lead you down the hillside into the nuns' cemetery below. Here too are the graves of local residents, but the place is dominated by a row of tall stately muhōtō-type tombs belonging to former abbesses. You can then leave the cemetery through a narrow alley which comes out by the northwest corner of Eishō-ji's property.

Finally Jōkōmyō-ji, which is located in a cul-de-sac in a quiet residential area on the other side of the railway tracks. This Shingon temple was founded by Hōjō Nagatoki in 1252 and, unlike the case of some other Kamakura temples, its subsequent history is well documented. It owns many fine statues, outstanding among which are the seated Amida Triad. At the rear there is the tomb of Reizei Tamesuke, a famous poet of the Fujiwara family who died in 1328. But I am afraid that the ordinary visitor will see very little of all this—only the pond, the courtyard, and the outside of the two temple buildings are accessible. Also, from time to time, a friendly ginger cat. Never mind, Kamakura has so much to show and offer that we shouldn't be too disappointed about this.

Great Buddha

Kamakura	_30 min._	Great Buddha	_10 min._	
Station	_Bus: 10 min._	大仏		

Hase Kannon	_10 min._	Gongorō Shrine
長谷観音		金吾邸神社

GREAT BUDDHA In the spring of 1195, Yoritomo, accompanied by his wife Masako, his son Yoriie, and a glittering retinue, set out from Kamakura and traveled to the imperial capital at Kyoto. The purpose of the expedition was to confer with Emperor Go-Toba, consolidate Minamoto influence at court, put on a public display of might in the capital, and do some sightseeing. It was during this visit to Kyoto that Yoritomo went to nearby Nara and attended the grand rededication ceremony at Tōdai-ji.

During the upheavals before Yoritomo won supreme command, the hall housing the Great Buddha of Nara and other Tōdai-ji buildings had been burned down in 1180 by Taira Shigemori, an impious act of infamy that, in the view of many, had incurred divine wrath and brought about the agitated death of Kiyomori (Shigemori's father) in the following year and the fall of the Taira clan soon after. Despite other pressing financial obligations, Yoritomo had generously supported the rebuilding of the temple razed by his enemies, although whether he had done this out of a genuine spirit of piety or rather to win the friendship of the powerful Buddhist hierarchy in the capital region can only be conjectured.

While in Nara for the solemn ceremony, attended by Go-Toba and most of the court, Yoritomo had the time and opportunity to inspect the colossal statue of Vairocana Buddha, sixteen meters in height and dating from the year 749. It was on this occasion (so it is plausibly suggested) that he conceived the idea of embellishing his own Kamakura headquarters with a similar imposing monument. It cannot be known for certain whether this Nara visit did in fact serve as an inspiration to erect the Great Buddha of Kamakura, for the large statue there was not constructed for more than fifty years after Yoritomo's death.

According to records, Idano no Tsubone, a lady-in-waiting at the Kamakura court, was the driving force behind the campaign to raise the necessary funds. Both she and the monk Jōkō spent years collecting money for the project, and finally, in 1238, work was begun on a big wooden statue. The construction took five years, for it was not until 1243 that the statue and hall were finished. But all this labor was brought to nothing a few years later, for a storm wrecked the monument in 1248 and fund raising was begun again.

This time the statue was to be made of more permanent material and was cast in bronze. After several unsuccessful attempts, work was completed in 1252 by a man about whom we know nothing save his name, Ōno Goroemon, and the statue was raised in a temple called Kōtoku-in. Lady Idano survived this happy event by only one year. Her memorial stone is appropriately set immediately behind the giant statue and tells us that she died on 1 July 1253.

Few visitors ever bother to learn the name of this small temple as it is generally referred to as "the Daibutsu," but actually the place has an extremely long religious history. Back in 741 the reigning emperor designated a head temple for each province, and the one for Sagami, in which Kamakura was located, was on the present site of Kōtoku-in. Not only that, but this particular temple was listed as the head temple for all the thirty-three provinces of eastern

Japan. So although the Great Buddha of Kamakura itself dates back only to the thirteenth century, the precincts in which the statue is located have had Buddhist connections for more than twelve hundred years.

The new Great Buddha was at first housed in a spacious hall, but it was not long before further disaster struck. Violent storms in 1335 and 1368 wrecked the building, and then in 1495 a tidal wave swept up the Hase valley and demolished the structure. Dozens of the stone foundations on which the wooden pillars of the hall rested can still be seen today both inside and outside the modern colonnade encircling the statue, and they give us some idea of the considerable size of the structure.

Since that time the Great Buddha has remained seated calmly and serenely in the open; the Japanese term *roza* often used when talking about the statue is rather fine, for it literally means "seated amid the dew." Various moves have been made in the past to rebuild the hall and replace the statue once more between four walls and a roof. But most visitors, whether pilgrims or tourists, would surely agree that it is far preferable to leave the monument seated amid the dew, with the green trees of the hill behind acting as a natural backdrop, rather than box it up again in a building.

Characteristically, the Kamakura statue depicts not Vairocana of the esoteric Kegon sect (as does the one in Nara), but Amida Buddha, the principal object of worship of the Jōdo and Shinshū sects, both of which developed in Japan during the early Kamakura period. Just as the mental discipline of Zen was considered highly suitable for warriors and nobles, so the popular and easy-to-understand doctrine of the new Amida sects attracted commoners and peasants. The essence of the Amida doctrine is that man is intrinsically incapable of obtaining salvation and entering paradise by his own unaided efforts. Instead, he must place his complete love and trust in Amida Buddha, whose infinite mercy and merits will ensure the salvation of even the wicked. In times of war, pestilence, famine, and other natural disasters, this was indeed a doctrine of hope and consolation, and it is small wonder that the Amida sects, although for historical reasons not well represented in Kamakura, rapidly spread and today make up the largest Buddhist grouping in Japan.

It is difficult to decide whether the Great Buddha of Kamakura should be admired more from the technological point of view or from the artistic. Casting with such exactness the large and heavy horizontal sections and then brazing them together (just *how* these sections were brazed together remains a bit of a mystery) called for a skill of extremely high order. The clever use of perspective should also be noted. Larger-than-life figures run the risk of appearing to be out of proper proportion, because parts of such large statues will necessarily be considerably further away from the spectator's viewing point and will therefore appear to be disproportionately small. Thus the pillars of some Greek temples, far from tapering at the top, were actually made imperceptibly thicker so that the entire column would appear to have a uniform diameter.

This principle is much in evidence in the Great Buddha. The head of the statue is disproportionately big when compared with the lower parts of the body. When viewed from the sides and the back, the figure looks unattractively hunch-shouldered and ungainly. Yet seen from the correct position, that is, four or five meters in front of the pedestal, these displeasing features completely vanish, and all appears in perfect harmony and proportion.

It is true that the Great Buddha in Nara is both taller (by some five meters) and older (by some five hundred years), but the Kamakura statue is generally considered the finer piece of work. In any case, the statue in Nara has been patched and repaired so often (the head fell off during an earthquake in 855, and the statue was melted when Shigemori's men burned down the hall in 1180; it was again destroyed by fire in 1567) that relatively little of the original work remains.

In contrast, the Great Buddha of Kamakura has remained unscathed and intact throughout its long history, despite the

The Great Buddha of Kamakura. ▷

damage suffered by the buildings enclosing it. In the Great Kantō Earthquake, the figure rocked dangerously back and forth, and according to an eyewitness one more tremor would have brought the statue toppling down to the ground. Happily it remained erect, although the left cheek of the face was slightly damaged and traces of the subsequent repair work can still be seen.

The forward-inclining head establishes an intimate feeling of relationship between statue and spectator, unlike the dusty and dimly lit Nara Great Buddha, whose remote blank eyes stare out to infinity some fifteen meters above the insignificant humans standing in front of the pedestal. The serene, passionless features of the Kamakura statue and the graceful fall of its robes give the figure, despite its 93-ton bulk, an air of delicacy and lightness. The rhythmic symmetry of the robe, incidentally, points to an indirect Greek influence, for asymmetry is characteristic of Japanese art and culture (as can be seen, for example, in painting, flower arrangement, and traditional gardens).

Long before the Europeans first arrived in Japan in the middle of the sixteenth century, Western artifacts and ideas had reached the country via the famous Silk Road that linked East and West through northern Asia. As a result of Alexander the Great's conquests in central Asia during the fourth century B.C., the Hellenic state of Bactria had been set up in what is now Pakistan. Artists working there fused Western and Eastern cultures by producing magnificent Buddhist figures looking for all the world like Greek statues with the flowing, stylized folds of their robes. This is very much apparent in the wonderful statue still preserved in Gokuraku-ji (page 132), only a couple of kilometers or so from the Great Buddha.

Further Greek influence can be discerned in some of the features of the face of the Great Buddha—the line of the eyebrows and nose, for example. It is strange to reflect that the indirect effects of Alexander's military campaigns should have reached as far as Japan and are still plainly visible, cast in bronze, in this statue.

Behind the Great Buddha are four large bronze lotus petals. They were made more than two centuries ago with the plan of seating the statue on a throne of petals after the fashion of the Nara Great Buddha. But twenty-eight more of these petals would be needed to implement the plan, and it seems unlikely now that anything will come of the idea.

Statistics are dull things, heaven knows, but I suppose that no account of the Great Buddha of Kamakura would be considered complete without including some facts and figures. The actual statue, not counting the base on which it is seated, is 11.4 meters high, while its circumference around the knees is 29.4 meters; as mentioned above, it weighs about 93 tons. There are 656 stylized curls on the massive head, and the silver boss in the forehead weighs 13.6 kilos; this boss, rather charmingly called a "fleshly excrescence" in some guidebooks, symbolizes the Buddha's mission to emit light and thus illuminate the entire world. The elongated earlobes, a common feature in Buddhist paintings and statues, indicate sanctity, and the lightly touching hands represent steadfast contemplation.

On payment of a modest fee, the visitor may enter inside the statue through a small door set below its left knee and inspect the cavernous, roughly finished interior. It has always seemed to me a great pity that this is allowed. After all, the tourist does not visit the Louvre to see the *Mona Lisa* and then demand to see the less than attractive back of the canvas. In the same way, the graceful Great Buddha was constructed as a religious and artistic masterpiece, and it is something of a desecration to let chattering tourists clamber noisily around the inside.

But this exercise in bad manners is nothing new (photographs taken in Meiji times even show men in kimonos and straw hats posing on the knees and hands of the statue), for some of the members of Captain John Saris's party went inside when the Englishman passed through Kamakura on his way back from Edo in 1613. This is what Saris, who went on to marry the daughter of the Lord Mayor of London on his return to England, had to say about the monument:

> The Countrey betwixt Surunga and Eddo is well inhabited. We saw many Fotoquise [*hotoke*, Buddhist deities] or Temples as we passed, and amongst others one Image of especiall note, called Dabis [Great Buddha], made of Copper, being hollow within, but of a very substantiall thicknesse.
>
> It was in height, as wee ghessed, from the ground about one and twentie foot, in the likenesse of a man kneeling upon the ground, with his buttockes resting on his heeles, his arms of wonderful largenesse, and the whole body proportionable.
>
> He is fashioned wearing of a gown. This image is much reverenced by Travellers as they passe there. Some of our people went into the bodie of it, and hoope and hallowed, which made an exceeding great noyse. We found many Characters and Markes made upon it by Passengers, whom some of my Followers imitated and made theirs in like manner.

Three years later, in 1616, Richard Cocks went to see the Great Buddha and in his enthusiasm exaggerated its size when he came to write up his diary.

> But that which I did more admire then all the rest was a mighty idoll of bras, called by them Dibotes [Great Buddha], and standeth in a vallie betwixt 2 mountaynes, the howse being quite rotten away, it being set up 480 years past [in fact, only 364 years].
>
> This idoll is made siting cros legged (telor lyke) and yet in my opinion it is above 20 yardes hie and above 12 yardes from knee to knee. . . . I doe esteem it to be bigger then that at Roads, which was taken for 1 of the 7 wonders of the world. . . . In fine, it is a wonderfull thinge.

At the risk of appearing chauvinistic, perhaps I may be allowed to add one more description, or rather appreciation, written by another Englishman—Basil Hall Chamberlain, who first arrived in Japan in 1873 and became one of the West's most learned and discerning scholars as regards things Japanese.

Chamberlain considered the Great Buddha of Kamakura to be "the greatest example of Japanese bonze-casting," and recommended repeated visits in order to gain a full appreciation of the statue, ". . . for like Niagara, like St. Peter's, and several other of the greatest works of nature and of art, it fails to produce its full effect on a first or even on a second visit; but the impression that it produces grows on the beholder each time that he gazes afresh at the calm, intellectual, passionless face. . . ."

My own personal experience bears out the truth of Chamberlain's remarks. The more you visit the Great Buddha, the more beautiful it appears, the more meaningful its message. Often enough, especially on weekends and public holidays, scores of people mill around the statue, either taking souvenir photos or forming up for the inevitable group portrait, but the noise and bustle hardly seem to matter. In fact they only serve to further emphasize the feeling of serenity imparted by the enigmatically half-smiling figure. Amida Buddha looks down on tourist and pilgrim alike with a calm (but not cold), loving, peaceful expression, and whatever one's religious beliefs or lack of them, the Great Buddha has something to teach us all.

HASE KANNON A kilometer or so from the Great Buddha is located the ancient Hase-dera, or Hase Temple, which houses an even older statue. The gilded standing figure of Kannon is 9.3 meters in height and is reputed to be the tallest wooden statue in the whole of Japan.

Kannon is usually, but somewhat loosely, described in English as "the Buddhist goddess of mercy," although, strictly speaking, the object of worship is neither masculine nor feminine. Kannon is Avalokitesvara Bodhisattva (a Bodhisattva is a future Buddha, destined for enlightenment, who in many cases has vowed to save all sentient beings), and represents compassion, mercy, and love. The cult of Kannon is immensely popular in Japan, and numerous stories in medieval literature attest to the efficacy of the deity's miraculous and merciful intervention on behalf of earnest suppliants.

The Hase statue is of the *jūichimen,* or eleven faces, type. With its overpowering wealth of symbolic decoration and its elongated form, the statue lacks the personal appeal of the nearby Great Buddha. Despite Kannon's merciful compassion, the figure gives an impression of aloofness and coldness. This impression is accentuated by the modern lighting system in the new hall. In former days the statue was not on continual display, and when shown to visitors, it was dimly lit by flickering lanterns.

As a result, more than one visitor left on record the eerie and awesome impression caused by the towering image. Lafcadio Hearn, for example, describes a visit he made to Kamakura in 1891 when he was taken to see the Hase Kannon. He groped his way into a pitch-black hall, and then an elderly monk attached two lanterns to suspended ropes and slowly raised the dim lights to the lofty ceiling. As the lanterns ascended, parts of the giant statue were momentarily illuminated, only soon to disappear once more into the darkness. The climax was reached when finally the disembodied face of Kannon emerged from the blackness, "smiling with eternal youth and infinite tenderness." Alas, all of this dramatic effect is lost in the modern, well-lit, and often noisy hall.

The statue is said to date back to the eighth century, when, in 721, a pious monk called Tokudō discovered a large camphor tree in the mountain forests near the village of Hase in the Nara region. He saw that the trunk of the great tree would make excellent material for a statue, and he managed to obtain the support of Fujiwara no Fusasaki, a high-ranking minister, in the project.

The tree was in fact so tall that its trunk provided sufficient material for two large statues, and the image carved from the lower part was enshrined in Hase village. In time a very popular cult grew around this statue and the temple housing it became a favorite place of pilgrimage, with both courtier and commoner traveling to Hase to plead for Kannon's merciful intercession. The temple is often mentioned in medieval Japanese literature, and even today the remote shrine, situated on the top of a hill and approached by a series of roofed flights of stairs, is an immensely popular center of devotion.

So much for the statue made from the lower half of the camphor trunk. According to legend, an even taller statue was carved from the upper part, and then cast into the sea near present-day Osaka and allowed to drift away to seek its own divinely appointed resting place (a variant of this story says that the upper part of the trunk was launched to sea uncarved, but no matter). The first place at which it was washed ashore was evidently not an auspicious spot. The statue brought bad luck to all who touched it, and so it was pushed out to sea again to get rid of its malign influence.

The much-traveled statue finally reached Yuigahama beach in Kamakura bay in 736 (fifteen years after its first launching), and this was to be its final destination. In the presence of Fusasaki, representing the empress, the Kannon was duly enshrined at a nearby place, which in view of the statue's origin came to be called Shin Hase, or New Hase. In the course of time, the name was abridged to simply Hase, and this part of Kamakura is still called Hase to this day.

Apart from the dominating Kannon statue, the interior of the main hall is crowded with a clutter of rather dusty statues and relics. On the left, in a miniature wooden shrine, sits a statue of Tokudō, the monk responsible for the creation of the statue. Other larger statues, such as the two Niō kings that I saw on visits many years ago, are no longer on view. But at the time of writing, a display hall is being built to the left of the main temple building, and it may well be that more of the temple's fine statues will be shown once more to the public in the near future.

To the right of the main building is a small shrine housing a golden seated statue of Yakuyoke (Protector-from-Evil-Spirits) Amida Buddha, one of Kamakura's six principal statues of Amida. The figure was commissioned by Yoritomo when he was forty-six years of age, that is, in 1194. Notice the ema, many of them featuring a horse, hanging to the left of the entrance. Most of them are signed, and they ask for a variety of favors—health, prosperity, happiness, success in examinations, and the finding of a suitable boyfriend. The one that appealed to me most on a recent visit read: "Health and happiness to all who pass through this temple." Amen to this touching and kindly petition.

Further to the right is found the temple bell dating back to the thirteenth century; according to an inscription on the bell itself, it was cast on 8 August 1264. The bell is Kamakura's third largest, after those of Engaku-ji and Kenchō-ji.

The garden at the foot of the steps leading up to the temple is pleasantly laid out with a fountain, pond, various grottoes, and a rather uninteresting cave. Should you enter the cave, be careful to mind your head. Painful experience teaches that violent contact with the low-lying roof can produce a headache that will spoil the rest of the day's tour.

One final point. Notice the Thousand Jizō on the flat area halfway up the steps. Actually there are probably many more than a thousand of these little statues, perched side by side in confused profusion. Many of them are wearing red, yellow, or blue bibs and caps, and some are clutching toy windmills. The overall effect is rather sweet and very touching. Probably most of these miniature statues were placed here by couples either to ask Jizō for the gift of a child, or a safe birth, or else to thank him for a safe birth, or to beg for the cure of a sick child. Whenever little children are concerned, Jizō is the deity to approach with confidence.

The annual Menkake parade at Gongorō Shrine.

GONGORŌ SHRINE   This small, usually deserted shrine is dedicated to the memory of Gongorō Kagemasa, a descendant of
Emperor Kammu; hence its popular name, although its official title
is Goryō Shrine. It would hardly be worth mentioning in this
general account, but for the fact that once a year, on 18 September,
Gongorō Shrine suddenly comes to life and stages a rather remarkable parade.

Unlike the rather stately processions organized during
Kamakura's principal festivals, this small shrine's outing is far
more of a local, homey affair. It often starts unpunctually, and
one solitary policeman is enough to escort the procession safely
over the tracks of the Enoshima Railway and through the narrow
streets of the vicinity.

The usual small portable shrines and drums are carried, but
what distinguishes this event are the eleven men wearing costumes
and grotesque, comical masks. One mask represents a long-nosed

bird, another a glaring red-faced demon, while a third fearsome creation has wild staring eyes with two Dracula-like fangs protruding from its mouth.

But the star of the show is undoubtedly the seventy-year-old gentleman wearing a black hood and a mask depicting a chubby-faced, vacant-looking woman. The man's midriff is generously padded below his sash to make him look as if he is in the last stages of pregnancy. Should the point be missed by spectators (and it is rather difficult to see how it *could* be missed), he repeatedly pats his ample stomach to draw attention to his (her?) condition. Legend has it that this character will help to ensure pregnancy and an easy childbirth, and so occasionally women and giggling young maidens reach out and touch the protruding girth.

Of course, there has to be story to explain this extraordinary parade. It is said that Yoritomo, who undoubtedly had a soft spot in his heart for comely young ladies, became intimate with a girl entertainer and in due course she found herself "in an interesting condition," as classical Japanese literature delicately describes such cases. As a result of the liaison, the girl's family was allowed to join the shogun's retinue when he visited Gongorō Shrine, but were obliged to wear masks to hide their lowly status. Hence the name of the outing—*menkake gyōretsu,* or face-hiding procession.

Fortunately, you don't have to believe this convenient but farfetched explanation to enjoy the light-hearted mini-festival as the parade meanders around the streets amid a good deal of joking and jostling between the weirdly masked characters and the local spectators. The procession is scheduled to start off in the early afternoon and is preceded by a performance of traditional *kagura* dancing in the shrine precincts.

Enoshima and
the Way Thither

Kamakura Station (Enoden Line)	*Train: 10 min.* →	Gokuraku-ji 極楽寺	*15 min.* →
Inamuragasaki 稲村ケ崎	*25 min.* →	Manpuku-ji 満福寺	*10 min.* →
Ryūkō-ji 竜口寺	*15 min.* →	Enoshima 江ノ島	

THE SOUTHERN PART of Kamakura lies open to the sea. It would be pleasant to relate that visitors can stroll along a broad, tree-lined promenade by the golden sands and blue sea, enjoying the fine view and fresh air. It would be pleasant indeed, but it wouldn't be true. Kamakura's seashore, so replete with historical memories, is little short of a disaster. The narrow beach, with its grayish sand, is poorly maintained and even squalid in places; run-down buildings and overgrown plots of land can be seen at intervals along the front; the volume of traffic down the inadequate coastal road increases by the year; at places there is not even a sidewalk, and pedestrians take their lives in their hands and walk along the side of the road. As for the traffic density—unless you have the patience of

Job and all the time in the world to spare, never travel by car or bus along the seashore on a summer weekend. It's quicker to walk.

Or to travel by the Enoshima Railway, affectionately called the Enoden (short for Enoshima Kamakura Kankō Densha), the sixth railway to be built in Japan and now the third oldest still in operation. Work began on this railway at the beginning of this century, although not without opposition from local rickshaw men, who, fearing this new form of competition, tore up parts of the track as soon as it was laid down. But construction work went ahead, and the first part of the line, running from Fujisawa to Katase, was opened on 1 September 1902. It was not until 1910 that the ten-kilometer track was finally completed, linking Kamakura to Fujisawa via Enoshima. The trains used to start from Wakamiya Avenue, but in 1949 the terminus was shifted to its present location within Kamakura Station.

The first part of the trip, that is, from Kamakura to Enoshima, along the single-track line is by far the most interesting. Not only does the train run along the seashore for long stretches, but the very names of the tiny stations en route—Gokuraku-ji, Inamuragasaki, Koshigoe—conjure up historical memories. The winding route is full of interest as the two-car train squeezes between houses and edges its way around backyards. In fact, it seems to have a serious identity problem and cannot make up its mind whether it is a real train or just a glorified streetcar. It is obviously a train when it stops at regular stations and awaits the oncoming train so that it can proceed along the single track. And only a real train would pass through such a long tunnel as that at Gokuraku-ji when it leaves the city proper. But then it becomes a mere streetcar as it rattles importantly down the main street of Koshigoe, fussily clanging its bell at any careless motorist who dares to hamper its stately progress.

GOKURAKU-JI   After leaving Hase Station, the Enoden runs in front of Gongorō Shrine, enters a tunnel to pass under the line of hills that defended the western side of the city, and then stops at Gokuraku-ji. Gokuraku-ji literally means Heavenly Temple, but the few buildings close by the Enoden tracks give no idea of the former size and prosperity of this once-great monastic establishment. All that is now left are a few nondescript buildings set in a quiet garden. And the emphasis is on peace and quietness. A notice at the front gate says that the place is open only to worshipers and pilgrims, and that no photographs may be taken. The latter prohibition seems to be rather strictly enforced, but the groups of people you see wandering around the place are obviously neither worshipers nor pilgrims.

The temple was founded at nearby Fujisawa in 1113, but was transferred to the present location, for reasons unknown, in 1259 under the patronage of Hōjō Shigetoki. In the time of its prosperity, Gokuraku-ji was an extremely large and flourishing establishment, and an ancient sketch map shows some fifty subtemples grouped around the main building. A pagoda was completed in 1315 and a Golden Hall six years later in 1321. But the inevitable natural disasters repeatedly struck the place and caused damage and destruction—fires in 1275 and 1425, and a major earthquake in 1433.

The Kyoto courtier Lady Nijō visited the temple in 1289 and was impressed by the comportment of the monks, and this made her homesick for the capital. Coming from Kyoto, she took the conventional view of Kamakura, however: the city was altogether unattractive in her eyes, and she comments on the shabby appearance of the nobles attending the shogun as he alighted from his litter at the Drum Bridge in front of Hachiman Shrine.

One, if not the principal, reason for Gokuraku-ji's early fame was its abbot Ninshō, who first came to the temple in 1267 and died in 1303. He is famed even to this day for his concern for the poor and the sick. The temple is said to have treated more than 50,000 patients during his tenure of office and became popularly known as the Lepers' Temple. The abbot not only organized this humanitarian work, but also took an active role in caring for the sick; to the right in front of the main building can be seen a large stone pestle and mortar that he used for grinding drugs and medicine.

Ninshō was also involved in public works and built 71 roads and no less than 189 bridges. He is even credited with cutting the Gokuraku-ji Pass, one of the traditional seven entrances into the city, enabling the local inhabitants to travel conveniently into central Kamakura. Small wonder, then, that the name of this good man was held in reverence and that an impressively large tomb was erected to his memory.

This handsome monument now lies outside the temple precincts, to the left of the playground belonging to the primary school behind Gokuraku-ji. Its quiet setting and noble proportions make it a fitting resting place for this great man, especially in the late autumn when the overhanging trees carpet the area with yellow and red leaves. In former times, you could visit the tomb without any difficulty or formality, but in recent years the path leading to the spot has been firmly barred with a metal gate and a strong padlock. Although a notice says that applications for the key should be made to the temple and so access is not completely forbidden, I can't help wondering whether the kindly Ninshō would have approved. He doesn't sound the sort of man who would favor padlocks and keys.

The tomb is almost four meters in height and is of the five-tiered type, consisting of five components each signifying one of the natural elements. Starting from the bottom, there is a cube (representing earth), then a sphere (water), pyramid (fire), crescent (air), and finally, on the top, a ball (emptiness or space). The tomb is reputed to be the tallest in Kamakura; this may be true, but the tombs in Myōhon-ji and Kōmyō-ji are not much shorter.

Some of the temple's treasures are preserved and displayed in the fireproof building on the right within the precincts. There are fine statues of a seated Shaka Nyorai, a fearsome Fudō, and the ten emaciated disciples of the Buddha on view. But Gokuraku-ji's principal statue is represented only by a large monochrome photograph. This is the superb wooden standing statue of Shaka Nyorai, the historical Buddha, and is put on display only once a year in April.

The slim figure stands one-and-a-half meters in height, palms outstretched, the right hand pointing upwards, the left downwards, in the gesture signifying fearlessness. Much of the spectator's appreciation can be lost by not knowing the statue's rich symbolism. Take the beautifully fashioned hands, for example. It is said that when a drunken elephant charged at the Buddha, he stopped and subdued the animal by simply raising his right hand toward it. Hence the symbolism of fearlessness. Later legends recount that five lions appeared from the five fingers and defended the Buddha from the elephant. The fearlessness displayed by the Buddha on this occasion sprang from his courage and tranquility, and so this gesture can also symbolize these two qualities. But in East Asian tradition, the hand gesture can also signify the preaching of the Law, especially the Buddha's sermon in the Deer Park in Benares. All this rich symbolism can be read into the simple gesture of the hands.

But the most striking feature of this lovely statue is the simple robe that clothes the figure. The swirling contours and symmetrical patterns of its folds impart an indescribable air of grace and delicacy. It is truly an object of great beauty, a beauty that is perhaps enhanced by the fact that it can be admired only once a year.

INAMURAGASAKI   Gokuraku-ji is set a little inland from the seashore; nearby, Inamuragasaki (or Inamura Point) juts out into the sea, with the Yuigahama beach to the east and the Shichirigahama beach to the west toward Enoshima. The line of hills runs straight into the sea and thus presented a formidable barrier to anybody approaching Kamakura from the west. In time of war, the narrow Gokuraku-ji Pass could be easily sealed off and

Inamuragasaki Point, site of the miraculous intervention in 1333.

defended, and the few feet of dry land (no longer existing) at the foot of Inamuragasaki cliff could likewise be barricaded.

The imperial troops sent to capture Kamakura in 1333 tried to enter through Gokuraku-ji Pass; fighting raged there for some time, but they made little progress and suffered heavy casualties. It was then that the commander of the expedition, Nitta Yoshisada, climbed to the top of Inamuragasaki cliff, raised his gold-decorated sword, and hurled it into the sea below, begging the gods to come to the aid of the emperor's stalled army. His prayer was answered, and the sea flowed back for more than one kilometer, catching the defenders by surprise (hardly to be wondered at in the circumstances) and leaving the approach to Kamakura wide open. Nitta's troops raced around the former obstacle, stormed into the city, and crushed the Hōjō.

This remarkable event, which conveniently explains how the allegedly impregnable city was captured, is commemorated today by a large stone monument on which are described the details of the miraculous operation. Nearby, to the right, stands a monument of two bronze figures representing a young boy clinging to his older brother; this memorial is for the dozen boys who were drowned in January 1910 while returning from an excursion trip to Enoshima. As recently as 1960 the city turned Inamuragasaki into an attractive park, with fine views of the wave-pounded rocks below, Kamakura bay, Enoshima, and (occasionally) Mount Fuji. The sea now washes right up to the foot of the cliff, making it impossible for one to walk uninterruptedly along the beach all the way from Kamakura to Enoshima. The nearby cut through which the coastal road runs is modern.

MANPUKU-JI   The Enoden train passes through the town of Koshigoe and runs in front of the steps leading up to Manpuku-ji—another nondescript-looking temple, but one that is firmly embedded in Japanese folklore. For it was here in Koshigoe in 1185 that Yoshitsune was ordered by his half brother Yoritomo to stop and not proceed any further into Kamakura. The young warrior languished at Koshigoe for some weeks, sending in appeals and declarations of loyalty, but Yoritomo, his suspicions inflamed by the calumnies of one of his lieutenants (who had fallen out with Yoshitsune on an earlier military campaign), adamantly refused to let him enter the city.

In desperation, Yoshitsune composed the *Koshigoe Letter,* one of the most famous missives in Japanese literature. The letter is dated 4 July 1185 and is addressed to one of Yoritomo's officials, although obviously intended for the general himself. In moving detail, Yoshitsune lists the dangers and hardships he has experienced while fighting for the Minamoto cause; he protests his complete loyalty toward his brother, pleading with him to relent and allow him to enter Kamakura; he describes his present sad predicament—"What can I do but weep bitter tears?"

Yoritomo is also supposed to have wept tears on reading the letter, but the appeal was in vain. In fact, sometime later the lord of Kamakura ordered a band of warriors to go and kill Yoshitsune.

And so began the young man's tragic odyssey, always on the run, always in hiding from his brother's dreadful vengeance.

In popular dramatic and literary representation, Yoritomo is mostly depicted as the cold-hearted tyrant, brutally hunting down his kith and kin, while Yoshitsune appears as the romantic victim of harsh but inexorable fate. Whether or not this accurately sums up the characters of the two brothers is difficult to say. Certainly, Yoritomo had a ruthless side to his character, but the same may be said of all the successful warriors of his time—if they weren't ruthless, they weren't successful.

But even Yoritomo balked at the prospect of viewing his brother's severed head. After Yoshitsune had committed suicide in 1189, his head was struck off, pickled in sakè, and transported over a long distance to Kamakura for inspection. Instead of going himself, Yoritomo sent two subordinates to identify the grisly relic.

Despite their positive identification, it was rumored that the dashing Yoshitsune had escaped to Ezo (Hokkaido), where he was deified and had shrines built in his honor. Another legend claims that he fled to China and became none other than the celebrated Genghis Khan, grandfather of Kublai Khan, whose troops twice attacked Kyushu, in 1274 and 1281, thus hastening the downfall of the Kamakura regime.

Small wonder, then, that the insignificant Manpuku-ji tends to make a great deal of Yoshitsune's sojourn in its precincts back in 1185. To the rear of the temple there is a spring, and this, of course, is where Yoshitsune used to wash. And the Benten pond to the right is called Suzuri (Inkstone) Pond, from which Yoshitsune obtained water for his inkstone when he came to write his famous letter. As for the letter itself, the temple will show on request a document reputed to be the original, but this is straining visitors' credulity a little bit too far.

RYŪKŌ-JI   A little beyond Manpuku-ji, the Enoden train trundles down the main street of Koshigoe and, just before it reaches

Enoshima Station, it passes in front of a Nichiren temple bearing the name Ryūkō-ji, the Temple of the Dragon's Mouth. This is an interesting temple complex and, unlike so many other temples in the Kamakura district, usually shows a good many signs of activity and life.

It will be recalled that, exasperated by his criticism of the government, the Hōjō rulers condemned Nichiren to death in 1271, and the monk was led off to the public execution site at Koshigoe. The execution date was fixed for 12 September. But just as the appointed swordsman was about to deliver the fatal stroke, a bolt of lightning descended from heaven and shattered his sword in two. The unusual phenomenon understandably gave the shaken executioner pause and delayed the proceedings. A messenger hurried back to Kamakura to relay the news, and on his way to the city he met at a stream another messenger bearing a writ of commutation. The stream in question is still known as Yukiaikawa, the Meeting Stream, and it runs to the east of Shichirigahama Station on the Enoden Line. Nichiren's death sentence was reduced to exile and he was sent off to Sado.

The followers and admirers of the patriarch obviously wished to commemorate his miraculous delivery from death, and in 1337 they built this temple on the execution site. The actual site is to be seen to the left of the front gate, before you climb the steps into the temple compound. The gate at the bottom of the steps is an indifferent piece of work, completed in recent years to mark the 700th anniversary of Nichiren's reprieve.

But the older gate at the top of the flight of steps is a fine example of Japanese woodcraft at its best. Notice on either side the ingenious panels on which are carved different scenes on the front and on the back. In the temple precincts, there is a bell and belfry on the right-hand side, and close by a modern statue of Nichiren. Near to this statue is a small stone marker on which is inscribed Hyakudō, or the Hundred Rounds; pilgrims making this set number of rounds about the temple receive special merit. The monks' quarters and administration offices to the right have a very fine and complex roof that is well worth studying.

A noteworthy feature of Ryūkō-ji is the number of pigeons that are always much in evidence in the grounds. They are both tame and greedy, and whenever a visitor, often a little child accompanied by a doting grandparent, casts his bread upon the ground, dense flocks of pigeons descend and start gobbling up the food. Should anybody then strike the temple bell or make any other alarming noise, the ensuing flurried panic is like a scene from Hitchcock's film *The Birds*.

The main building is one of the largest temple halls in the Kamakura district and may be freely entered. As usual with Nichiren temples, golden decorations hang down from the ceiling in profusion. Some caves to the left of the building are reputed to have been used to imprison Nichiren while he was awaiting execution. A path to the right of the main building leads up the hill behind the temple and brings the visitor to a fine five-storied pagoda. Built in 1910, the pagoda may be approached close up so that a full appreciation of the intricate woodwork can be obtained. This wooden structure and the main hall were the only buildings in Ryūkō-ji to survive the Great Kantō Earthquake.

If visitors follow the path a little further and then look back, they will be able to admire the Japanese genius for blending the works of man and nature into a satisfying intrinsic harmony, for the unpainted wooden pagoda merges without effort into the background of tall trees.

Which is more than can be said about the startling white structure nearby. Built in traditional Siamese style to commemorate the 700th anniversary of Nichiren's deliverance, the tower is intended to house Buddhist relics. The aesthetic contrast between the two buildings, one gently harmonizing into its natural surroundings, the other stridently and discordantly sticking out, is significant. So often when building in traditional style with traditional materials Japanese craftsmen produce a thing of beauty; but

The pagoda at Ryūkō-ji.

when they turn to unfamiliar and foreign patterns, the finished product can leave an awful lot to be desired.

Ryūkō-ji's annual festival is observed on 11–13 September, when not only the temple grounds but also the surrounding streets are jammed with pilgrims who have come as far away as Tokyo to observe the anniversary of Nichiren's escape from death. Many of the faithful carry hand drums that they beat rhythmically to the endless chant of *Namu Myōhōrengekyō,* the sect's invocation in honor of the *Lotus Sutra.* Throughout the night the crowds mill around, the people chant, the drums beat, the clouds of scented incense rise. It's an impressive sight and an almost hypnotic experience.

ENOSHIMA   Finally we reach Enoshima, the small hilly wooded island linked to the shore by a long bridge. As so often the case of Japanese offshore islands, Enoshima has been regarded from time immemorial as a place of religious significance. The cult of Benten, always associated with water, is particularly prominent here. The well-kept shrine consists of three main buildings and is usually thronged with visitors even on weekdays. Various famous people in Japanese history, for example, Yoritomo in 1182, have come to Enoshima to offer prayer and petition to the gods. The place appears to have been inhabited for thousands of years, as pre-historic remains have been discovered on this island.

As in so many similar places, the mixture of sacred and profane is much in evidence in Enoshima. Crowds come every weekend to inspect the fresh shellfish on sale in the stalls along the bridge, visit the innumerable souvenir shops (all seem to sell exactly the same gaudy items) on either side of the road winding up the steep hill, enjoy the fine sea views, and visit the shrine.

The climb to the top of the island is arduous, although facilitated in recent years by the installation of a long, four-stage escalator. But the view from the higher parts of the island are well worth the effort of climbing, for visitors can look down from the cliffs on to the rocks, waves, and birds far below. It is a good idea to have something to eat or drink in one of the restaurants by the edge of the cliff facing east (that is, toward Kamakura), for it is often possible to sit on an overhanging balcony and look down on the scene below—and this includes an extensive yachting marina, from which the 1964 Olympic yachting trials were held. Right at the very top of the island is a tropical plant park and a less-than-handsome observation tower.

One of the most famous landmarks of this fascinating little island is now no longer open to the public. This is the Benten Cave on the far side of the island, but in recent years the sanctuary has been closed owing to the danger of falling rocks. I well remember the first time I entered this cavern—the sound of trickling water

echoing along its pitch-black interior and the ghostly outlines of
the statues of various deities dimly perceived in the flickering glow
of a totally inadequate torch made this an unforgettable experience. An underground passage is said to run from the cave all
the way to the crater of Mount Fuji, some eighty kilometers away
and splendidly visible from Enoshima on clear days. Well, perhaps
so, but if there really is such a passage, it must be the world's
longest tunnel.

Hiking Courses

Gion-san Course;   Great-Buddha Course;   Ten'en Course
祇園山コース   大仏コース   天園コース

THERE ARE VARIOUS interesting walks along the paths through the
hills surrounding Kamakura, and these are called Hiking Courses
(in Japanese, *haikingu kōsu*). On the whole they are fairly well
signposted, and it is difficult to lose your way. Some sections can be
a little steep and the going a bit rugged, but the paths can be easily
followed by anybody who is active and in reasonably good health.
I have taken dozens of groups through the hills, and so far
everybody has happily survived the ordeal. Sometimes it has
happened that just as we are, weary and sweaty, clambering up a
slope, we have been overtaken by a band of little old ladies, clad in
kimono and resolutely bearing staves, chattering and laughing
among themselves as they passed us youngsters. And then there
was the occasion when I was negotiating a steep path in a remote
part of the hills and I ran into a man wheeling a bicycle. . . .

One point to bear in mind is that quite a few of the paths serve as
water courses in wet weather, and so walks through the hills are not
recommended within a day or two of heavy rain. All apart from the
mud and puddles, the slopes can become very slippery and, in
places, potentially dangerous.

Another factor to bear in mind about these walks is that the paths not only afford splendid views of the city and countryside but also have considerable historical interest. Some of them in fact must date right back to the Kamakura period or even earlier, as is shown by the ancient burial caves you come across along the way. From earliest times people have obviously followed the easiest way when going from A to B, and this is precisely what these paths offer as they meander along the natural contours of the hills. The only difference is that in olden days these routes were used by people precisely to get from A to B. Nowadays they serve only as enjoyable hiking courses for recreation, and they can take you pretty well from one end of Kamakura to the other along scenic paths without crossing a modern, traffic-clogged road. There are three principal hiking courses that can be recommended.

GION-SAN COURSE This path is the shortest of the three and possibly the least interesting one; it runs from south to north along the top ridge of Gion Hill, more or less parallel to Wakamiya Avenue. You can pick up the path either at Yagumo Shrine (just to the right of the shrine building) or a little further along the way at Myōjon-ji. At the latter place there are two ways of joining the track, either by the path to the right just before you ascend the steps leading to the main gate of the temple, or by the path winding up the hill on the right as you enter the cemetery to the left of the main temple building.

As you walk along this hiking course, from time to time you will catch glimpses of the city center down below you on the left. Eventually you begin a steep descent and come out by the Harakiri Cave (page 40). You can, of course, make the walk in the other direction, but let the voice of experience recommend you not to do so. Both here and in the walks described below I give the direction that is easier to follow.

GREAT-BUDDHA COURSE   This is a particularly lovely route, and on weekdays it is usually quite deserted. The course begins in Kuzugahara Park, just above Zen'i-arai Benten (page 108), and there are various ways of reaching this starting point. You can walk from the station to Zen'i-arai Benten, continue up the steep road for about a hundred meters, and the course begins on the left; it is clearly signposted. Or you can walk from Kita-Kamakura Station and reach Kuzugahara Park by taking the path by the side of Jōchi-ji and going up the Kewaizaka Pass. Finally, you can pick up the path leading from the de Becker tomb in Jufuku-ji cemetery (page 103), and this will bring you to the park. Or if you wish to visit the Sasake no Inari Shrine first, take the path leading up past the shrine buildings, pass under the large fallen tree trunk that arches over the route, and at the top of the hill you will come out a little way along the Great-Buddha Course.

It takes about thirty to forty minutes from one end of this course to the other. Toward the end look out to the left, and you will see the Hase valley leading down to the sea and the Great Buddha seated in Kōtoku-in far below. A long flight of irregular steps takes you eventually down to the road running into the Great-Buddha Tunnel; walk for ten minutes or so *away* from this tunnel and you will reach the Great Buddha.

TEN'EN COURSE   This is by far the longest of these three courses, and it runs through the hills to the north of the city (that is, behind Hachiman Shrine), from the eastern parts of Kamakura to Kita-Kamakura. The whole of this hilly region is designated loosely as Ten'en, Heavenly Park. Sometimes the pretentious name "Kamakura Alps" is found in tourist maps and gives the impression that oxygen masks, ice picks, and stanchions are standard equipment for anybody planning this trip. In reality, the loftiest hill is no more than 150 meters in height.

For various reasons, it is better to walk along this path from east to west, rather than in the reverse direction. The easternmost entrance is reached by a path going from Junisō Shrine (page 69), but a nearer one is found to the right of the first gate in front of Zuisen-ji (page 52). I myself usually take visitors past Kamakura Shrine and climb into Ten'en by the path that begins on the right just a hundred meters or so before you reach Kakuon-ji (page 55). If you use this last entrance into Ten'en, notice the burial caves to the right of the path before it joins the trail running from east to west across the line of hills. Many of these caves in Kamakura are located in inaccessible places, but these particular ones can be easily reached from the path.

Halfway along this trail, and near some more burial caves, you will come across an iron observation platform set a few steps above on the right-hand side. Here you will enjoy a magnificent view of Kamakura—the wooded hills stretch out on either side, and you can see Hachiman Shrine, Wakamiya Avenue running down to the sea, and the whole of the city spread out below you.

At the end of the trail more steps lead down into Hansōbō, a small temple in the hills behind Kenchō-ji. It is sometimes described as a "mountain goblin temple," and there used to be metal statues of these mountain goblins in the grounds before they were taken away and melted down as part of the war effort (you can see similar statues today in the shrine on Mount Takao to the west of Tokyo). This small temple used to be part of Hōkō-ji in Shizuoka, but was transferred to the present site as recently as 1890. It observes a festival on the seventeenth day of each month, and it attracts a surprisingly large number of visitors. More steps take you down through the pleasant precincts, and then a path running between cherry trees leads to the rear of Kenchō-ji.

The above are the three recognized hiking courses in Kamakura, but there are plenty of other worthwhile walks in and around the city. I would recommend the Asahina Pass (page 69) for those wishing to get away from it all and make a quiet walk into the heart of the countryside. The path running by Jōchi-ji (page 32) will provide you with an enjoyable stroll into Kuzugahara Park. Then there is a path from Chōshō-ji leading down into Zaimokuza and coming out in the maze of lanes near Kōmyō-ji. Or else why not take the Kamegayatsuzuka Pass as a shortcut between Kita-Kamakura and the city center. And the walk from the Harakiri Cave (page 40), through the long Sannōgayatsu Tunnel, then through the Shakadō Tunnel, and so on to Sugimoto-ji is an interesting trip.

The Seven Passes

Gokuraku-ji Pass; Great-Buddha Pass; Kewaizaka Pass;
極楽寺切通し　　　　大仏切通し　　　　　化粧坂切通し

Kamegayatsuzaka Pass; Kobukurozaka Pass;
亀ケ坂切通し　　　　　巨福呂坂切通し

Asahina Pass; Nagoe Pass
朝比奈切通し　　名越切通し

As I NOTED IN the introductory chapter, the hills surrounding Kamakura on three sides made the city an easy place to defend against outside attack. The city was considered so impregnable that a miraculous intervention had to be introduced to explain how Nitta Yoshisada's troops managed to storm the city in 1333. But for more than a century Kamakura was a political center and had to maintain viable lines of communication with the rest of the country, especially with Kyoto. And so there were recognized passes that led into and out of the city, and these are called the *nana-kiridōshi,* the seven passes. These entrances were strictly guarded, and close by there were usually inns where travelers could stay. In fact, as the weary traveler passed through the checkpoints, he was sometimes greeted by a bevy of young ladies soliciting him to stay at their inns. The following list begins with the pass to the southwest of the city.

GOKURAKU-JI PASS In olden days there was apparently a narrow strip of beach around the Inamuragasaki bluff, but it was impractical for large numbers of people to enter the city at this point. And so the Gokuraku-ji Pass, located a little inland, was frequented by travelers approaching the city along the coastal route. It is said to have been constructed by Gokuraku-ji's benevolent abbot, Ninshō. Whether he (or other people) made this cut from scratch, or whether a natural break in the hills was widened and enlarged, is not known. When Masako entered Kamakura in 1180, she passed around the Inamuragasaki bluff, so presumably this more convenient route had not yet been opened by that date. A walk through the narrow defile gives you a good idea of the ease with which this entrance could be defended. In the 1333 attack on Kamakura, one-third of the assault forces were deployed at this place and heavy fighting raged for several days.

GREAT-BUDDHA PASS Formerly known also as the Fukazawa Pass, this entrance connected with the road to Fujisawa. It did not, of course, pass through the present long tunnel, which was first opened in 1880, but crossed over the hill to the west of the tunnel.

KEWAIZAKA PASS When you look at this remote slope nowadays, it is hard to realize that this was one of the most important entrances into Kamakura. It was bitterly contested in the 1333 fighting, although one is free to believe or not the *Taiheiki* version, according to which no less than 600,000 horsemen attacked this vital pass. Incidentally, *Kewai* is written with two characters usually read in combination as *keshō,* meaning "cosmetics," so the name can be translated as "Cosmetics Slope." They say that the place got its odd name because the severed heads of the defeated Taira warriors were brought into Kamakura through this entrance, and before being officially inspected and identified here, these grisly trophies were duly washed and touched up with cosmetics.

KAMEGAYATSUZAKA PASS   This entrance has a much more pleasing name, even though it is a little long (it is easier to assimilate when divided up as Kame-ga-yatsu-zaka). It literally means Tortoise Valley Slope, for the slope is so steep that even tortoises cannot climb it. I wasn't aware that tortoises are supposed to be good climbers, but never mind. This pleasant, quiet lane can be still used as a shortcut between Kita-Kamakura and the city center. You will notice how narrow the route becomes in places, and so it could easily be defended. Notice also the Kōfū-en hotel hidden away through a tunnel. Together with Kewaizaka Pass, this route was important, as it served traffic coming from Musashi.

KOBUKUROZAKA PASS   The modern road passes through a cut made in the Meiji era, but the old trail used to run slightly to the west. If you walk along the narrow road beginning near the west entrance of Hachiman Shrine, you will see traces of the former pass. An old shrine is perched high up to the left, while *dōsōjin* monuments, dedicated to the deities of the wayside, can be seen here and there. The lane peters out into private property, making it impossible to follow this old pass along the entire way. This pass is thought to date from about 1240 and may have been constructed on the orders of Hōjō Yasutoki, the third regent, but nothing certain is known.

ASAHINA PASS   This is a beautiful route, and has already been described (page 69). This east entrance into Kamakura was important because it served the traffic from Kanazawa, and food supplies from the farming districts of Chiba were brought in through Asahina Pass. Its name is said to originate from one Asahina Yoshihide Saburō, whose mother was the formidable Tomoe Gozen, a woman renowned for her strength and bravery in battle. In this respect the herculean Saburō seems to have taken after his mother, for such was his mighty physique that he singlehandedly cut this pass in one night—an extraordinary feat in those pre-bulldozer days. According to a more sober account, the road was opened by Hōjō Yasutoki, who himself supervised the operation and even helped to carry away earth and stones in 1241, just one year before his death.

NAGOE PASS   The road tunnel now in use is, of course, modern, and the old route appears to have run over the top of the present railway tunnel. There was a very ancient road here, and it is even mentioned in the eighth-century *Kojiki,* which says that Yamato-takeru, third son of Emperor Keikō, followed this route during his military campaign against the Ebisu barbarians in the east of Japan.

Restaurants and Shops

HOWEVER MUCH INTERESTED you may be in Kamakura's temples, shrines, history, and culture, the time will come during your visits to think about some food and drink. There are literally scores of restaurants and cafes in and around the city, and it is relatively simple for the foreign visitor to obtain lunch and refreshment at the ordinary places, especially those serving Western food. There are a number of attractive private residences that have been converted into restaurants, and for the most part they serve only traditional Japanese food. Although it is an interesting and instructive experience for the foreigner to eat at such places, it may be as well on the first visit to be accompanied by a Japanese-speaking friend to advise you on menu, cost, and customs.

Among these traditional restaurants, an outstanding example is Tori-ichi [とり一, 1–4–16 Ōgigayatsu; tel. (0467) 22–1818], tucked away in a secluded valley on the way to Zen'i-arai Benten. A leisurely lunch in a private room overlooking the traditional Japanese garden is a delightful experience and much to be recommended for special occasions. The menu is written entirely in Japanese, but photographs will help you to choose your order. Tori-ichi is closed on Tuesdays, and advance reservations are necessary.

Another place much to be recommended is the Chinese restaurant Kaseirō [華正樓, 584 Hase; tel. (0467) 22–0280], located on the left-hand side of the road as you approach the Great Buddha. Advance reservations are advisable for parties of more than five or six people.

Perhaps the best plan for anybody making a casual visit to Kamakura is to patronize the restaurants in the center of the city, especially those in Komachi-dōri, the road running parallel to Wakamiya Avenue and beginning from the red torii archway in the far left-hand corner of the plaza in front of Kamakura Station's eastern entrance. As you walk along Komachi-dōri, you will find Nanura-en 南浦園 (Chinese) and Komachi 小満ち (*tonkatsu*) on the left-hand side. A little further to the right is Komachi Dō-biru 小町銅ビル, which has three restaurants on the first floor and a sandwich bar on the second. Also on the right is Zum-zum ズムズム, a second-floor restaurant that serves reasonably priced steaks. On the left, Nakamura-an 中村庵 provides excellent *soba* dishes. For those who can made do on sandwiches and salad, there is Hakuraiya a little further on the left. Coffee shops, selling drinks, ice cream, cakes, and light snacks abound along this street and do not require any specific introduction.

Along Wakamiya Avenue, on the way to Hachiman Shrine, McDonald's offers prompt service to the hungry hiker—takeout on the first floor, restaurant on the second. By the large torii midway along the avenue, there is the Ni no Torii Biru 二ノ鳥居ビル, with the Yamazato 山里 (Japanese food) on the first floor, and Ni no Torii (general Western food) on the second. This is an interesting block as you will find in quick succession the shops Akari あかり (folkcrafts), Wakami-ya 和歌美屋 (Kamakura-bori, or dark-red lacquered wooden goods), and Torii-ya 鳥居屋 (folkcrafts).

Visitors will often wish to buy presents and souvenirs, and here again Komachi-dōri has plenty of interesting shops to satisfy most tastes. As you walk from the station, you will see on the left-hand side Takayama 高山 (art), Shatō 社頭 (folkcrafts and wonderful *washi,* or Japanese paper), Yamato 大和 (folkcrafts), and Kamaya かまや (folkcrafts). On the right-hand side of the road, Takahashi 高橋 is an interesting shop exhibiting a variety of traditional wooden artifacts.

Perhaps the best souvenir or present from Kamakura is Kamakura-bori, but such items are often expensive. There are more than a dozen shops selling this specialized ware, and they are scattered in different parts of the city. For the sake of convenience, I would recommend a visit to the area at the end of Wakamiya Avenue, immediately in front of Hachiman Shrine, for here you will find five Kamakura-bori shops located close together. Yōgadō 陽雅堂 is situated on the left-hand corner, while on the opposite side of the road there are Hakkōdō 博古堂, Azumaya 吾妻屋, Anzai 安斉, and Hashōdō 八勝堂, all within fifty meters of each other. Whether you buy anything or not, you may walk around these shops and inspect the displayed goods at your leisure.

Wakamiya Avenue is also lined with many antique shops offering all kinds of traditional Japanese items. In the hills above Zen'i-arai Benten is located the House of Antiques, run by Mr. Yoshihiro Takishita. Here Japanese antiques of the medium price range and up are beautifully displayed in a 300-year-old farmhouse. The shop is open by appointment only [tel. (0467) 43–1441], and English is spoken.

Principal Annual Events

JANUARY

1–3 New Year visits to Hachiman Shrine and Kama-
kura Shrine.

5 New Year's archery at
Hachiman Shrine.

25 Burning of *fude* (writing
brushes) at Egara Tenjin.

FEBRUARY

3 Bean-throwing at spring
equinox at Hachiman
Shrine and Kamakura
Shrine.

12 Cold-water penitential
rite at Chōshō-ji.

MARCH

17–18 Hansōbō festival.

APRIL

3 Festival at Wakamiya
Shrine in Hachiman
Shrine.

3–4 Commemorative services
for Hōjō Tokimune at
Engaku-ji.

7–14 Kamakura Festival. Historical parade on second
Sunday of month.

8 Buddha's birthday at
temples.

13 Service at Yoritomo's
tomb.

MAY

28 Festival at Shirohata
Shrine in Hachiman
Shrine.

JUNE

1–14 Hydrangea display at
Meigetsu-in.

3 Festival at Kuzuharaga-
oka Shrine.

20 Enoshima-Kamakura sea

festival. (Date is approximate.)

JULY

7 Yagumo Shrine festival.
14 Enoshima sea festival.
25 Egara Tenjin festival.

AUGUST

7–9 Lantern festival at Hachiman Shrine.
10 Black Jizō festival at Kakuon-ji.
15 Festival of the Dead (Bon) at temples.
20 Festival of Kamakura Shrine.
23–24 Foundation ceremonies at Kenchō-ji.

SEPTEMBER

1 Festival of Myōhon-ji.
2–3 Foundation ceremonies at Engaku-ji.
9 Gokuraku-ji festival; Jūniso Shrine festival.
11–13 Festival at Ryūkō-ji.

14–16 Autumn festival at Hachiman Shrine.
16 *Yabusame* (mounted archery) at Hachiman Shrine.
18 *Menkake* (Face-Hiding) parade at Gongōrō Shrine.
22 Torch-light Noh at Kamakura Shrine.
30 Commemoration of Musō Kokushi at Zuisen-ji.

OCTOBER

9 Ryūkō-ji festival.
10–15 Kōmyō-ji festival.

NOVEMBER

1–3 Kenchō-ji and Engaku-ji *mushiboshi* display of treasures.
15 7–5–3 festival at Hachiman Shrine and Kamakura Shrine.

DECEMBER

17–18 Hase-dera festival.
31 *Joya no kane* bell ringing at temples.

Index of Temples, Shrines, and Places

MICHAEL COOPER first came to Japan in 1954 as a student and spent two years studying Japanese at a language school near Kamakura. Ever since then he has been a confirmed Kamakura buff, and in fact the notes taken during his student days form the basis of the present guidebook. In between prowling around Kamakura and showing groups of visitors the historical sites, he edits *Monumenta Nipponica,* the quarterly journal of Japanese culture, at Sophia University, Tokyo. He is also author of *Rodrigues the Interpreter* (Weatherhill, 1974).

The "weathermark" identifies this book as a production of John Weatherhill, Inc., publishers of fine books on Asia and the Pacific. Editorial supervision: James T. Conte. Book design and typography: Meredith Weatherby and James T. Conte. Production supervision: Yutaka Shimoji. Composition, platemaking, and printing, in offset, by Komiyama Printing Company, Tokyo. Bound at the Okamoto Binderies, Tokyo. The typeface of the main text is Monophoto Times New Roman in ten-point size.

To Yokohama
and Tokyo

Kita-Kamakura
Station

Ten'en Course

i Pass
ha Pass
Pass
suzaka Pass
aka Pass
ss

D
C
E
F

Great-Buddha
Course

B

A

Kamakura
Station

Gion-san
Course

Ebisudō
Bridge

Geba
Bridge

Moto-
Hachiman

Midare
Bridge

Yokosuka
Line

G

To Zushi

Yuigahama

Enoden Line

Wakamiya Avenue

Komachi-dōri

Nameri River

Hase
Wadazuka

Gokuraku-ji

gasaki

Yuigahama Beach

Sagami Bay

miho

N

KAMAKURA